George Franklin Bowerman

A selected bibliography of the religious denominations of

the United States

George Franklin Bowerman

A selected bibliography of the religious denominations of the United States

ISBN/EAN: 9783337261719

Printed in Europe, USA, Canada, Australia, Japan

Cover: Foto ©Lupo / pixelio.de

More available books at **www.hansebooks.com**

A SELECTED BIBLIOGRAPHY

OF THE

RELIGIOUS DENOMINATIONS

OF THE UNITED STATES

COMPILED BY

GEORGE FRANKLIN BOWERMAN

B. A., B. L. S.

———

WITH A

LIST OF THE MOST IMPORTANT CATHOLIC WORKS OF THE WORLD AS AN APPENDIX

COMPILED BY

REV. JOSEPH H. McMAHON

———

NEW YORK
CATHEDRAL LIBRARY ASSOCIATION

———

1896

PREFACE.

This list is designed to furnish a guide to the study of the churches and religious denominations of the United States. This purpose is best served by a selected list rather than by a complete bibliography. It aims to present to the student, in systematic form, references to the best books on the history, doctrines and polity of each church. Wherever year-books or journals of conferences are published by a denomination or in its interest, these are recorded as furnishing valuable statistical information. A few of the most eminent or most representative weekly journals and the leading church reviews are included. In all cases where obtainable, publisher, place and date of publication and price have been given.

It is thought that this little list will be of value to clergymen, theological seminaries and Christian workers generally. In attempting to give to each student a list that will not only help him to understand his own denomination better, but will guide him to the best that has been written about other denominations, my underlying purpose has been to contribute something to church union, and still more to Christian unity.

Attention is called to the appendix, in which is given a very excellent list of the most important Catholic books of the world. It would be a little aside from the plan of my work to include these books in my list, which is strictly confined to the United States. Feeling, as I did, that my list, which on this church includes only American publications, would inadequately represent its splendid literature, I was fortunate in interesting Father McMahon in my work, and in inducing him to prepare the list which he has given.

In making this compilation I have made use of the bibliographical helps mentioned elsewhere. Of these, I have probably derived most help from those scattered through the volumes of the American Church History Series, and especially from the alphabetical list compiled by Samuel Macauley Jackson, D. D., which is given in volume 12 of that series. The work on my list was mostly done at the New York State Library at Albany, which has a good collection of books on American religious history.

Material about the smaller denominations has been hard to obtain since records of their books do not often appear in the trade bibliographies. In the case of many of them I have been able to give fairly good lists, and this has been made possible by the ready response of denominational publishers who have sent me books, and clergymen who have sent me manuscript bibliographies of their denominations.

For help in my work, then, I am indebted to a large number of clergymen and publishers all over this country. Even though I do not here mention them, to each of them I am thankful.

GEORGE F. BOWERMAN.

NOTE.

The order of arrangement is such that allied bodies are grouped together under the most general heading, *e. g.*, Seventh-day Baptists are grouped with Baptists instead of being put in strict alphabetical order after the Shakers. By entering denominations under their various headings in the index each one may be readily found. The general sources of information, such as bibliographies and other books of reference, are given first.

v.

SELECTED BIBLIOGRAPHY

OF THE

RELIGIOUS DENOMINATIONS

OF THE UNITED STATES.

GENERAL WORKS.

GENERAL BIBLIOGRAPHY.

Crooks, G. R., *D. D.* and Hurst, J. F., *D. D.* Histories of the Christian Churches in the United States, [1894]. (in their Theological Encyclopædia and Methodology, 1894. pp. 597–610).

Classified by denominations ; fragmentary.

Hurst, J. F., *D. D.* Bibliotheca Theologica: a Select and Classified Bibliography of Theology and General Religious Literature. 417 pp., 8°. N. Y., Scribner's Sons, 1883. $3.

———— Literature of Theology: Classified Bibliography of Theological and General Religious Literature. 757 pp., 8°. N. Y., Hunt and Eaton, 1895. $4.

Based on his Bibliotheca Theologica.

Jackson, S. M., *D. D.* Bibliography of American Church History, [1894]. (American Church History Series, v. 12, pp. 441–513).

A straight alphabetical list by authors.

———— A Ministerial Library, [1893]. (see Schaff's Theological Propædeutic, 1893. pp. 537–96).

GENERAL CYCLOPÆDIAS.

Jackson, S. M., *D. D.,* Chambers, T. W., *D. D.* and Foster, *Rev.* F. H. Concise Dictionary of Religious Knowledge and Gazetteer. Ed. 3. 996 + 45 pp., maps, 4°. N. Y., Maynard, Merrill & Co., 1893. $4.

McClintock, John, *D. D.* and Strong, James, *D. D.* Cyclopædia of Biblical, Theological and Ecclesiastical Literature. 10 v. and 2 v. supplement, il., maps, 4°. N. Y., Harper & Bros., 1883–88. $5 each.

Schaff, Philip, *D. D.*, *ed.* Religious Encyclopædia; or,
Dictionary of Biblical, Doctrinal and Practical Theology,
Based on ... Herzog, Plitt and Hauck ... with an Encyclopædia of Living Divines. Ed. 3, enl. 4 v., 48+2629+
296 pp., 4°. N. Y., Funk & Wagnalls, 1891. $5 each.

These three are all rich in bibliographies and contain good brief
articles descriptive of the religious denominations of the United
States.

GENERAL HISTORY AND STATISTICS.

Belcher, Joseph, *D. D.* Religious Denominations in
the United States, Their History, Doctrines. Government
and Statistics. New ed. 1024 pp., il., 4°. Phil., J. E. Pot-
ter & Co., 1861.

Good for statistics at time it was published.

Carroll, H. K., *D. D.* Religious Forces of the United
States. 62+449 pp., 8°. N. Y., Christian Literature Co.,
1893. (American Church History Series, v. 1). $3.

Author was in the charge of the 11th census ; besides putting
the statistical matter in very available shape, he also gives information about minor bodies which is nowhere else to be found.

—— *Compiler.* Report on Statistics of Churches in
the United States at the 11th Census, 1890. 27+812 pp.,
pl., 4°. Wash., Government Printing Office, 1894. *Free
to libraries.*

Dorchester, Daniel, *D. D.* Christianity in the United
States, from the First Settlement down to the Present
Time. New ed. enl. 814 pp., il., 8°. N. Y., Methodist
Book Concern, 1895. $3.50.

First published in 1887 ; in this edition all data brought down to
close of 1894.

Nippold, F. Americanische Kirchengeschichte seit Un-
abhängigkeitserklärung der Vereinigten Staaten. 272 pp.,
8°. Berlin, Wiegandt & Schotte, 1892. (v. 4 of his
Handbuch der Neuesten Kirchengeschichte). 6.40 marks.

DOCTRINES.

Crooks, G. R., *D. D.* and Hurst, J. F., *D. D.* Theological Encyclopædia and Methodology, on the Basis of Hagenbach. New ed. 627 pp., 8°. N. Y., Methodist Book Concern, 1894. $3.

Contains many valuable bibliographies, including lists of denominational histories, pp. 597–610.

Schaff, Philip, *D. D.* Theological Propædeutic: a General Introduction to the Study of Theology . . . Including Encyclopædia, Methodology and Bibliography. 596 pp., 8°. N. Y., Scribner's Sons, 1893. $3.

A highly satisfactory work : rich in bibliography.

——Bibliotheca Symbolica Ecclesiæ Universalis: The Creeds of Christendom, with a History and Critical Notes. 3 v., 8°. N. Y., Harper & Bros., 1877. $15.

v. 1. History of Creeds.

v. 2. Greek and Latin Creeds.

v. 3. Evangelical Creeds.

Rich in bibliography ; up to time of its publication this work accurately represents the creeds of the various churches.

CHURCH UNITY.

Bradford, A. H., *D. D.*, *ed.* The Question of Unity; Many Voices Concerning the Unification of Christendom. 84 pp., 12°. N. Y., Christian Literature Co., 1894. 75 cents.

Shields, C. W., *D. D.* The Historic Episcopate: an Essay on the Four Articles of Church Unity Proposed by the American House of Bishops and the Lambeth Conference. 65 pp., 12°. N. Y., Scribner's Sons, 1894. 60 cents.

——The United Church of the United States. 285 pp., 8°. N. Y., Scribner's Sons, 1895. $2.50.

WORLD'S PARLIAMENT OF RELIGIONS, 1893.

Barrows, J. H., *D. D.*, *ed.* World's Parliament of Re-

ligions . . . held in Chicago . . . 1893.   2 v., 1600 pp., il.,
8°.   Chic., Parliament Pub. Co., 1893. $5.

Part 4, comprising the last 220 pages of v. 2, contains a brief account of some of the leading religious denominations.

Bonet-Maury, A. G. C. A.   The Congress of Religions
at Chicago in 1893.   346 pp., 14 portraits.   Paris, 1895.

Hanson, J. W., *D. D.*, *ed*.   World's Congress of Religions; Addresses and Papers Delivered before the Parliament and an Abstract of the Denominational Congresses.
1196 pp., il., 8°.   Chic., W. B. Conkey & Co., 1894. $2.75.

Houghton, W. R., *ed*.   Neely's History of the Parliament of Religions and Religious Congresses at the World's
Columbian Exposition.   1001 pp., il., 8°.   Chic., F. T.
Neely, 1894. $2.50.

Jones, J. L., *D. D.*, *ed*.   A Chorus of Faith as Heard
in the Parliament of Religions.   333 pp., 12°.   Chic., Unity
Pub. Co., 1893. $1.25.

Mercer, *Rev*. L. P., *ed*.   Review of the World's Religious Congresses, Chicago, 1893.   334 pp., il., 12°.
Chic., Rand, McNally & Co., 1893. $1.

Savage, *Rev*. M. J., *ed*.   World's Congress of Religions.   428 pp., 12°.   Bost., Arena Pub. Co., 1893. $1.25.

Stevens, C. M., *ed*.   World's Congress of Religions.
663 pp., il., 12°.   Chic., Laird & Lee, 1894.   Paper, 50 cents.

LAWS OF RELIGIOUS CORPORATIONS.

Humphrey, G. H.   Law of Protestant Episcopal Church
and Other Prominent Ecclesiastical Bodies : a Manual for
Church Officers, with Forms.   Ed. 4. enl.   226 pp., 12°.   N.
Y., Jas. Pott & Co., 1895. $1.50.

Hunt, Sanford, *D. D.*   Laws Relating to Religious Corporations: a Compilation of the Statutes of the Several
States in the United States.   273 pp., 12°.   N. Y., Methodist
Book Concern, 1876.   *Out of print.*

Tyler, R. H. American Ecclesiastical Law: the Law of Religious Societies. 539 pp., 8°. Albany, Gould, 1866. $4.50.

ADVENTISTS.

SECOND ADVENTISTS.

History.

Wellcome, *Rev.* I. C. History of the Second Advent Message and Mission, Doctrine and People. 707 pp., 8°. Yarmouth, Me., Author, 1874. $2.50.

Doctrines.

Wellcome, *Rev.* I. C. and Goud, Clarkson. Plan of Redemption by Our Lord Jesus Christ. Ed. 8. 460 pp., 12°. Yarmouth, Me., Scriptural Publication Society, 1867.

Pettingell, J. H. The Unspeakable Gift. 365 pp., 12°. Yarmouth, Me., I. C. Wellcome, 1887. $1.00.

Periodical.

World's Crisis and Second Advent Messenger, weekly. Bost. $1.75.

NOTE.—Publishing house is now Scriptural Publication Society, Auburn, Me.

SEVENTH-DAY ADVENTISTS.

History.

Loughborough, *Rev.* J. N. Rise and Progress of Seventh-day Adventists. 392 pp., il. Battle Creek, Mich., Review and Herald Pub. Co. $1.25.

Doctrines.

Andrews, J. N. History of the Sabbath and the First Day. Ed. 2. 348 pp. Battle Creek, Mich., Review and Herald Pub. Co., 1873. $2.00.

Periodical.

Advent Review and Sabbath Herald, weekly. Battle Creek, Mich. $1.00. Established 1850.

BAPTISTS.

(Including Baptists generally.)

Bibliography.

Crowell, W. Literature of American Baptists from 1814 to 1864. [1869]. (See American Baptist Missionary Union. Missionary jubilee. N. Y., 1869. pp. 391–461.)

History.

Armitage, Thomas, *D. D.* History of the Baptists Traced by Their Vital Principles and Practices from . . . Jesus Christ to ... 1886. 978 pp. il., 4°. N. Y., Bryan, Taylor & Co., 1887. $6.00.

Burrage, H. S., *D. D.* History of the Baptists in New England. 317 pp., 16°. Phil., American Baptist Pub. Soc., 1894. (Baptist History Series, v. 1.) $1.25.

Cathcart, William, *D. D.* Baptist Encyclopædia; a Dictionary of the Doctrines, Ordinances, Usages, Confessions of Faith. Sufferings, Labors and Successes. and of the General History of the Baptist Denomination in All Lands. 2 v. il., 4°. Phil., L. H. Everts, 1883.

Cramp, J. M., *D. D.* Baptist History to the Close of Eighteenth Century. 598 pp., 12°. Phil., American Baptist Pub. Soc., 1869. $1.75.

" Best popular book, but untrustworthy."

Moss, Lemuel, *D. D., ed.* Baptists and the National Centenary: a Record of Christian Work, 1776-1876. 310 pp., 8°. Phil., American Baptist Pub. Soc., 1876. $1.75.

——History of the Baptists in the Trans-Mississippi States. 16°. Phil., American Baptist Pub. Soc. *Announced.* (Baptist History Series, v. 5.) $1.25.

Newman, A. H., *D. D.* History of the Baptist Churches in the United States. 513 pp., 8°. N. Y., Christian Literature Co., 1894. (American Church History Series, v. 2.) $3.
Includes a five-page bibliography.

Smith, J. A., *D. D.* History of the Baptists in the Western States, East of the Mississippi. 16°. Phil., American Baptist Pub. Soc. *Announced.* (Baptist History Series, v. 3.) $1.25.

Sprague, W. B., *D. D.* Annals of the American Pulpit: Baptist. v. 6, 860 pp., 8°. N. Y., Carter & Bros., 1860. $4.

Vedder, H. C., *D. D.* History of the Baptists in the Middle States. 16°. Phil., American Baptist Pub. Soc. *Announced.* (Baptist History Series, v. 2.) $1.25.

———Short History of the Baptists. 245 pp., 12°. Phil., American Baptist Pub. Soc., 1891. 60 cents.

Williams, W. R., *D. D.* Lectures on Baptist History. 360 pp., 12°. Phil., American Baptist Pub. Soc., 1877. $1.75.

Doctrines and Polity.

Burrage, H. S., *D. D.* Act of Baptism in the History of the Christian Church.. 252 pp., 16°. Phil., American Baptist Pub. Soc., 1879. 90 cents.

Burrows, J. L., *D. D.* What Baptists Believe. 320 pp., 16°. Baltimore, R. H. Woodword & Co., 1893. 60 cents.

Hiscox, E. T., *D. D.* New Directory for Baptist Churches. 604 pp., 16°. Phil., American Baptist Pub. Soc., 1894. $1.50.

———Manual for Baptist Churches. 174 pp., 18°. Phil., American Baptist Pub. Soc., 1890. 40 cents.

Johnson, E. H., *D. D.* Outline of Systematic Theology, and of Ecclesiology, by H. G. Weston, *D. D.* Ed. 2.

383 pp., 8⁰. Phil., American Baptist Pub. Soc., 1895. $2.50.

Wilkinson, W. C., *D. D.* Baptist Principle in its Application to Baptism and the Lord's Supper. 252 pp., 12⁰. Phil., American Baptist Pub. Soc., 1881. $1.25.

Periodicals.

Central Baptist, weekly. St. Louis. $2. Established 1863.

Examiner, weekly. N. Y. $2. Established 1830.

Standard, weekly. Chicago. $2.50. Established 1853.

Watchman, weekly. Bost. $2.50. Established 1819.

Year-book.

American Baptist Year-book, 1868–date. 12⁰. Phil., American Baptist Pub. Soc. 25 cents.

FREE-WILL BAPTISTS.

History.

Burgess, G. A. and Ward, J. L., *D. D.* Free Baptist Cyclopædia. 724 pp., il. 4⁰. Minneapolis, Free Baptist Cyclopædia Co., 1889. $4.

Centennial Record of Free-Will Baptists, 1780–1880. New ed. 266 pp., 8⁰. Dover, N. H., F. B. Printing Establishment, 1881. $1.

Free-Will Baptists—General Conference. Minutes . . . 1827–86. 2 v. 12⁰. Dover, N. H., 1859, and Bost., 1887, F. B. Printing Establishment. $2.

Stewart. *Rev.* I. D., *ed.* History of the Free-Will Baptists for Half a Century, 1780–1830. v. 1, 479 pp., 12⁰. Dover, N. H., F. B. Printing Establishment, 1862. $1.

Williams, A. D. Memorials of the Free-Communion Baptists. 254 pp., 8⁰. Dover, N. H., F. B. Printing Establishment, 1873. $1.

Doctrines.

Butler, J. J., *D. D.* Christian Theology. 456 pp. Dover, N. H., F. B. Printing Establishment, 1861. $1.50.

Free-will Baptists—General Conference. Treatise on the Faith and Practices of the Free-will Baptists. New ed. 72 pp., 16°. Bost., F. B. Printing Establishment, 1894. 25 cents.

Free Communionist by Four Authors. 214 pp. Dover, N. H., F. B. Printing Establishment, 1841.

Periodicals.

Free Baptist, weekly. Minneapolis, Western F. B. Pub. Soc. $1.50. Established 1882.

Morning Star, weekly. Bost. $2. Established 1826.

Year-book.

Free Baptist Register and Year-book for 1825–date. Bost., Morning Star Pub. House. 20 cents.

Formerly published at Dover, N. H.

SEVENTH-DAY BAPTISTS.

History.

Bailey, *Rev.* James. History of the Seventh-day Baptist General Conference. 12°. Toledo, O., S. Bailey & Co., 1866. $1.50.

Clark, *Rev.* Henry. History of the Sabbatarians or Seventh-day Baptists in America.

Doctrines.

Lewis, A. H., *D. D.* Biblical Teachings Concerning the Sabbath and the Sunday. Ed. 2. 144 pp., 12°. N. Y., Amer. Sabbath Tract Soc., 1888. 60 cents.

———Critical History of Sunday Legislation from 221 to 1888. 279 pp., 16°. N. Y., Appleton & Co., 1888. $1.25.

Lewis, A. H., *D. D.* Critical History of the Sabbath and
the Sunday in the Christian Church. 583 pp., 16°. Alfred
Centre, N. Y., Amer. Sabbath Tract Soc., 1886. $1.25.

——Seventh-day Baptist Hand-book. 64 pp., 16°.
Alfred Centre, N. Y., Amer. Sabbath Tract Soc., 1887.
15 cents.

Periodical.

Sabbath Recorder, weekly. Plainfield, N. J., Amer-
Sabbath Tract Soc. $2. Established 1844.

The American Sabbath Tract Society is now located at Plainfield, N. J.

CHRISTIAN SCIENTISTS.

Doctrines.

Eddy, *Mrs.* Mary Baker Glover. Science and Health;
with Key to the Scriptures. Ed. 85. 663 pp., 8°. Bost.,
E. J. Foster Eddy, M. D., 1894. $3.18.

Periodical.

Christian Science Journal, monthly. Bost., Christian
Science Pub. Co. $2. Established 1883.

CHRISTIANS.

Summerbell, *Rev.* N. True History of the Christians
and the Christian Church, from 4000 A. M. to 1870 A. D.
8°. Cincinnati, 1871. (Dayton, O., Christian Pub. Association.)

CHURCH OF GOD (WINEBRENNERS).

Doctrines.

Forney, C. H., *D. D.* The Christian Doctrines. Harrisburg, Pa., Pub. House of Church of God. 75 cents.
Winebrenner, *Rev.* John. Doctrinal and Practical Ser-

mons. 402 pp. Harrisburg, Pa., Pub. House of Church of God. $1.50.

Periodical.

Church Advocate, weekly. Harrisburg, Pa. $2. Established 1835.

Year-book.

Year-book of the Church of God, 1888-90. 12°. Harrisburg, Pa., Pub. House of Church of God. 15 cents each.

Discontinued. These three numbers contain valuable statistics, brief biographies and other historical material.

CONGREGATIONALISTS.

Bibliography.

Dexter, H. M., *D. D.* Congregationalism of the Last 300 Years as Seen in its Literature ; with a Bibliographical Appendix. N. Y., Harper & Bros., 1880. $6.

Contains 308 pp. of bibliography.

Walker, Williston. Creeds and Platforms of Congregationalism. 604 pp., 8°. N. Y., Scribner's Sons, 1893 $3.50.

Including much bibliographical material and reprints of original documents.

History.

Bacon, Leonard, *D. D.* Genesis of the New England Churches. 485 pp., 8°. N. Y., Harper & Bros., 1874. $2.50.

Dexter, H. M., *D. D.* Congregationalism of the Last 300 Years as Seen in its Literature ; with a Bibliographical Appendix. 716+329 pp., 8°. N. Y., Harper & Bros., 1880. $6.

Dunning, A. E., *D. D.* Congregationalists in America :

a Popular History of their Origin, Belief, Polity, Growth, and Work.   552 pp., il. 8°.   N. Y., J. A. Hill & Co., 1894. $2.75.

Huntington, *Rev.* George.   Outlines of Congregational History.   201 pp., 12°.   Bost., Cong'l S. S. & Pub. Soc., 1885. $1.

Punchard, George.   History of Congregationalism from About 250 to the Present Time.   Ed. 3.   5 v., 12°.   Bost., Cong'l Pub. Soc., 1867-81. $10.

Volumes 4-5 have title, "Congregationalism in America."

Sprague, W. B., *D. D.*   Annals of the American Pulpit : Trinitarian Congregationalists.   V. 1-2, 8°.   N. Y., R. Carter & Bros., 1857. $8.

Walker, Williston.   History of the Congregational Churches in the United States.   451 pp., 8°.   N. Y., Christian Literature Co., 1894.   (American Church History Series, v. 3.) $3.

Includes a good bibliography, pref. pp. 9-13.

Doctrines and Polity.

Dexter, H. M., *D. D.*   Handbook of Congregationalism.   212 pp., 16°.   Bost., Cong'l Pub. Soc., 1880. $1.

Ladd, G. T.   Principles of Church Polity, Illustrated by an Analysis of Modern Congregationalism.   433 pp., 8°.   N. Y., Scribner's Sons, 1882. $2.50.

Ross, A. H., *D. D.*   The Church Kingdom : Lectures on Congregationalism.   386 pp., 8°.   Bost., Cong'l S. S. & Pub. Soc., 1888. $2.50.

Roy, J. E., *D. D.*   Manual of the Principles and Usages of the Congregational Churches.   48 pp.   Bost., Cong'l S. S. & Pub. Soc.   10 cents.

Walker, Williston.   Creeds and Platforms of Congregationalism.   604 pp., 8°.   N. Y., Scribner's Sons, 1893. $3.50.

Periodicals.

Bibliotheca Sacra, a Religious and Sociological Quarterly. Oberlin, O. $3. Established 1844.

Congregationalist, weekly. Bost. $3. Established 1817.

Advance, weekly. Chic. $2. Established 1867.

Kingdom, weekly. Minneapolis. $1.50. Established in 1888 with title, " Northwestern Congregationalist."

Pacific, weekly. San Fran. $2.50. Established 1851.

Year-book.

Congregational Year-book. 8⁰. Bost., Cong'l S. S. & Pub. Soc. $1.

Has been published since 1854.

DISCIPLES OF CHRIST (CAMPBELLITES).

History.

Hayden, A. S.   Early History of the Disciples in the Western Reserve, Ohio.   476 pp., 12⁰.   Cincinnati, Chase & Hall, 1876. $2.

Longan, G. W.   Origin of the Disciples of Christ.   12⁰. St. Louis, Christian Pub. Co., 1889.

Tyler, B. B., *D. D.*   History of the Disciples of Christ. 162 pp., 8⁰.   N. Y., Christian Literature Co., 1895. $1. (Also in American Church History Series, v. 12, pp. 1–162.)

Includes a one-page bibliography.

Doctrines.

Campbell, Alexander.   The Christian System, in Reference to the Union of Christians.   358 pp., 12⁰.   St. Louis, Christian Pub. Co. $1.50.

Garrison, *Rev.* J. H., *ed.*   The Old Faith Restated.   St. Louis, Christian Pub. Co., 1891.

Tyler, B. B., *D. D.* Peculiarities of the Disciples. Cincinnati, Standard Pub. Co.

Sermons.

Periodicals.

Christian Evangelist, weekly. St. Louis, Christian Pub. Co. $1.75. Established 1863.

Christian Standard, weekly. Cincinnati, Standard Pub. Co. $2. Established 1866.

Year-book.

Year-book of the Disciples of Christ. 8°. St. Louis Christian Pub. Co.

DUNKARDS (GERMAN BAPTIST BRETHREN CHURCH.)

Doctrines.

Brumbaugh, H. B. Church Manual. New ed. 64 pp., 24°. Mt. Morris, Ill., Brethren Pub. Co., 1893. 25 cents.

Miller, R. H. Doctrine of the Brethren Defended; or-The Faith and Practice of the Brethren. 404 pp., 12°. Indianapolis, Ind., German Bapt. Brethren Book and Tract Work, 1876. $1.25.

West, Landon. Close Communion; or, Plea for the Dunkard People. 192 pp., 16°. Dayton, O., German Bapt. Brethren Book and Tract Work, 1888. 25 cents.

Periodicals.

Gospel Messenger, weekly. Mt. Morris, Ill., Brethren Pub. Co. $1.50. Established 1863.

Year-book.

Brethren's Family Almanac. 8°. Mt. Morris, Ill., Brethren Pub. Co.

EPISCOPALIANS.

PROTESTANT EPISCOPAL CHURCH.

History.

Benham, *Rev.* W. Short History of the Episcopal Church in the United States. 148 pp. 1 por., 12°. Lond., and N. Y., E. P. Dutton & Co., 1884. 2s. 6d.

Benton, *Rev.* A. A. Church Cyclopædia: a Dictionary of Church Doctrine, History, Organization and Ritual. 810 pp., 8°. Phil., L. R. Hamersley & Co., 1884. $5.

Coleman, Leighton, *bp.* History of the Church in America. 8°. N. Y., James Pott & Co., 1895. $2.50.

McConnell, S. D., *D. D.* History of the American Episcopal Church from the Planting of the Colonies to the End of the Civil War. 392 pp., 8°. N. Y., Thomas Whittaker, 1890. $2.

Perry, W. S., *bp. comp.* Handbook of the General Convention of the P. E. Church, Giving its History and Constitution, 1785–1880. Ed. 3. 365 pp., 12°. N. Y., Thomas Whittaker, 1881. $2.

——History of the American Episcopal Church, 1587–1887. 2 v. il., 4°. Bost., J. R. Osgood & Co., 1885. $15.

—— *ed.* Historical Collections Relating to the American Colonial Church. 5 v. in 4, 4°. Hartford, Ct., Church Press Co., 1870–78.

v. 1, Virginia. v. 4, Maryland.
v. 2, Pennsylvania. v. 5, Delaware.
v. 3, Massachusetts.

Tiffany, C. C., *D. D.* History of the Protestant Episcopal Church in the United States. 8°. N. Y., Christian Literature Co., 1895. (American Church History Series, v. 7.) $3.

Wilson, J. G., and others. Centennial History of the P. E. Church in the Diocese of New York, 1785–1885.

454 pp., por., 8°. N. Y., D. Appleton & Co., 1886. $4.
Of more than local interest and importance.

Doctrines and Polity.

Protestant Episcopal Church in the United States.
Book of Common Prayer. 566 pp., 24°. N. Y., James
Pott & Co., 1892. 25 cents.

Huntington, W. R., *D. D.* Short History of the Book
of Common Prayer, with Papers Illustrative of Liturgical
Revision, 1878–92. 235 pp., 12°. N. Y., Thomas Whittaker, 1893. $1.

Little, *Rev.* A. W. Reasons for Being a Churchman. 266
pp., 12°. Milwaukee, Wis., Young Churchman Co., 1885.
$1.

Mason, *Rev.* A. J. The Faith of the Gospel: a Manual
of Christian Doctrine. 403 pp., 12°. Lond., Rivington,
1887. 7s. 6d.

Percival, H. R. The Doctrine of the Episcopal Church
as Set Forth in the Prayer-book. 163 pp., 12°. N. Y.,
Putnam, 1892. 75 cents.

Seabury, W. J., *D. D.* Introduction to the Study of
Ecclesiastical Polity. 304 pp., 12°. N. Y., Crothers &
Korth, 1894. $1.50.

Temple, E. L. The Church in the Prayer-book: a Lay-
man's Brief Review of Worship. 408 pp., 12°. Milwaukee,
Wis., Young Churchman Co., 1893. $1.20.

Periodicals.

Church Eclectic, monthly. 8°. Utica, N. Y. $3. Es-
tablished 1873.

Protestant Episcopal Review, monthly. Theological
Seminary, Fairfax Co., Va. $1. Established 1889. (Not
published in Aug. and Sept.)

The Churchman, weekly. N. Y., M. H. Mallory & Co. $3.50. Established 1844.

Living Church, weekly. Chicago. $2. Established 1878.

Southern Churchman, weekly. Richmond, Va., $2. Established 1883.

Year-books.

American Church Almanac and Year-book, 1830–date. 12°. N. Y., James Pott & Co. 25 cents.

Living Church Quarterly, Containing an Almanac and Calendar for 1886–date. 12°. Milwaukee, Wis., Young Churchman Co. 25 cents.

First number of every volume is almanac for year.

Protestant Episcopal Almanac and Church Directory for 1855–date. 16°. N. Y., Thomas Whittaker. 25 cents.

Protestant Episcopal Church in the United States— General Convention. Journal of the Proceedings.

REFORMED EPISCOPAL CHURCH.

History.

Aycrigg, Benjamin. Memoirs of the Reformed Episcopal Church and of the Protestant Episcopal Church. 66+373 pp., 8°. N. Y., Author, 1875. (Ed. 5, 1880.)

Article in McClintock and Strong's Cyclopædia of Biblical, Theological, and Ecclesiastical Literature.

Doctrines.

Reformed Episcopal Church. Prayer-book. Phil., Reformed Episcopal Pub. Soc. 40 cents.

Cheney, C. E., bp. What Do Reformed Episcopalians Believe? 193 pp., 16°. Phil., Reformed Episcopal Pub. Soc., 1888.

Periodicals.

Episcopal Recorder, weekly. Phil., Religious Press Assoc. $2.

Parish Messenger, monthly. Chicago.

Year-book.

Reformed Episcopal Church. Journal of the Proceeding of Council. Phil., Reformed Episcopal Pub. Soc. (For 1894 is 14th.)

EVANGELICALS.

EVANGELICAL ASSOCIATION.

History.

Breyfogel, S. C., *bp.* Landmarks of the Evangelical Association. Reading, Pa., Author, 1888.

Krobel, G. C., *D. D.*, *ed.* Congress of the Evangelical Association; a Complete Edition of the Papers Presented, September 19–21, 1893. 333 pp., 12°. Cleveland, Thomas & Mattill, 1894.

Spreng. *Rev.* S. P. History of the Evangelical Association., 1894. (See American Church History Series, v. 12, pp. 383–439.)

Includes a one-page bibliography.

Yeakel, R. History of the Evangelical Association. 2 v., 8°. Cleveland, O., Pub. House of the Evangelical Assoc., 1894–95. $4.

———Jacob Albright and his Co-laborers. 329 pp., 12°. Cleveland, O., Pub. House of the Evangelical Assoc. 1883.

Doctrines.

Evangelical Association of North America. Doctrines and Discipline. 179 pp., 16°. Cleveland, O., Pub. House of the Evangelical Assoc., 1893.

Periodicals.

Christliche Botschafter, weekly. Cleveland, O., Pub. House Evangelical Assoc. $2. Established 1836.

Evangelical Messenger, weekly. Cleveland, O., Pub. House Evangelical Assoc. $2. Established 1847.

Year-book.

Christian Family Almanac. 8°. Cleveland, O., Pub. House Evangelical Assoc.

UNITED EVANGELICAL CHURCH.

History.

Heil, *Rev.* W. F. United Evangelical Church. (See Independent, 3 Jan., 1895, p. 4.)

This body began life as a sect 28 Nov., 1894.

Doctrines and Polity.

United Evangelical Church. Doctrines and Discipline of the ... Church Formulated by the General Conference of 1894. 171 pp., 24°. Harrisburg, Pa. Bd. of Pub. of United Evangelical Church, 1895.

Periodical.

Evangelical, weekly. Harrisburg, Pa. $1.50. Established 1888.

Year-book.

United Evangelical Church. Journal of the General Conference, 1894. 8°. Harrisburg, Pa., Evangelical Pub. Co., 1894. 25 cents.

FRIENDS.

Bibliography.

Smith, Joseph. Descriptive Catalogue of Friends' Books, or Books Written by Members of the Society of Friends. 2 v., 4°. Lond., Author, 1867.

Smith, Joseph. Friends' Books: Supplement to a Descriptive Catalogue of Friends' Books. 364 pp., 4°.
Lond., E. Hicks, Jr., 1893. 20 s.

——Bibliotheca Anti-quakeriana; or, a Catalogue of
Books Adverse to the Society of Friends. 474 pp., 8°.
Lond., Author, 1873.

Swathmore College—Friends' Historical Library. Catalogue. 62 pp., 16°. Swathmore, Pa., 1893.

History.

Beck, William. The Friends. Lond., Edward Hicks,
Jr., 1893.

Bowden, James. History of the Society of Friends in
America. 2 v., 8°. Lond., A. W. Bennett, 1850-54. 19 s.

Gough, John. History of the People Called Quakers.
4 v. Dublin, Robert Jackson, 1790.

Hallowell, Richard P. The Pioneer Quakers. Bost.,
Houghton, Mifflin & Co., 1887. $1.

——The Quaker Invasion of Massachusetts. Bost.,
Houghton, Mifflin & Co., 1883. (Ed. 4, 1887.) $1.25.

Janney, S. M. Examination of Causes Which Led to
Separation of Friends in America in 1827–28. 350 pp.,
12°. Phil., Friends' Book Store, 1868. $1.

——History of the Religious Society of Friends from
its Rise to 1828. 4 v., 12°. Phil., T. E. Zell, 1859–67. $6.

Michener, Ezra. Retrospect of Early Quakerism.
434 pp., pl., 8°. Phil., T. E. Zell, 1860. $1.50.

Sewel, William. History of the Rise, Increase and
Progress of the Christian People Called Quakers. Ed. 2.
Lond., J. Sowle, 1725.

Speakman, T. H. Divisions in the Society of Friends.
Ed. 3 enl. 127 pp., 16°. Phil., J. B. Lippincott Co., 1896.
63 cents.

Thomas, A. C., and Thomas, R. H. History of the

Society of Friends in America. Phil., J. C. Winston & Co., 1895. (Also see American Church History Series, v. 12, pp. 163–308.)

Includes a good bibliography of seven pages. Professor A. C. Thomas is a member of the "Hicksites" and Dr. R. H. Thomas of the "Orthodox" branch of this denomination: so each branch is represented with fairness.

Townsend, Alice N. Chronology of the Society of Friends, 1644–1828. 12°. Phil., Friends' Book Assoc., 1895. 40 cents.

Turner, F. S. The Quakers: a Study Historical and Critical. 406 pp., 8°. Lond., W. S. Sonnenschein & Co., 1889. 6 s.

Friends' Congress (Liberal), 1893. Friends' Presentation in the Parliament of Religions and Proceedings in their Denominational Congress, 9th Month, 19–23. 147 pp., 8°. Chic., W. B. Conkey & Co.

Doctrines.

Barclay, Robert. An Apology for the True Christian Divinity as the Same is Held Forth and Preached by the People Called in Scorn, Quakers. Phil., Friends' Bookstore. (First printed in Latin, Amsterdam, Jacob Claus, 1676.)

Great standard of Friends.

Evans, Thomas. Exposition of the Faith of the Religious Society of Friends. 316 pp., 8° Phil., Kimber & Sharpless, 1827. 75 cents.

Evans, William & Thomas, *eds.* The Friends' Library, Comprising Journals, Doctrinal Treatises and Other Writings. 14 v. Phil., The Editors, 1837–50.

Rules and Discipline of the Yearly Meeting. 136 pp., 8° Phil., 1888.

Periodicals.

Orthodox.

American Friend, weekly, July 19, 1894–date.   Phil. $1.50.

The Friend, a Religious and Literary Journal, weekly, 1827–date. Phil. $2.

The two following have ceased publication:

Friends' Review, weekly.   Phil., 1847–94.

Christian Worker, weekly.   Phil., 1871–94.

Hicksite.

Friends' Intelligencer and Journal, weekly, 1844–date. Phil. $2.50.

GERMAN EVANGELICAL SYNOD.

History.

Shory, *Rev.* Albert. Geschichte der Deutschen Evangelischen Synode von Nord-America. 137 pp., il., 8° St. Louis, Verlag der Deutschen Evang. Synode, 1889. 5c cents.

Doctrines.

German Evangelical Synod of North America. Small Evangelical Catechism. 63 pp., 16°. St Louis, Verlag der Deutschen Evang. Synode, 1892. 15 cents.

Periodicals.

Der Freidensbote, semi-monthly. St. Louis. $1. Established 1849.

Theologische Zeitschrift, monthly, 1872–date. 8°. St. Louis. $2.

Year-book.

Evangelischer Kalender auf das Jahr. St. Louis, Verlag der Deutschen Evang. Synode. 15 cents.

JEWS.

History.

Daly, C. P. Settlement of the Jews in North America. 171 pp., 8°. N. Y., Philip Cowen, 1893. $1.50.

Markens, Isaac. Hebrews in America: a Series of Historical and Biographical Sketches. 352 pp., 8°. N. Y., Author, 1888.

Union of American Hebrew Congregations. Judaism at the World's Parliament of Religions, 1893. 418 pp., 8°. Cincinnati, Robert Clarke Co., 1894. $2.50.

Periodicals.

American Hebrew, weekly. N. Y., Philip Cowen. $3.

American Israelite, weekly. Cincinnati. $4. Established 1854.

Jewish Exponent, weekly. Phil. $3. Established 1883.

Year-book.

Union of American Hebrew Congregations. Annual Report, 1875–date. 8°. Cincinnati, Bloch Co.

LUTHERANS.

Bibliography.

Morris, J. G., *D. D.* Bibliotheca Lutherana: a List of Publications of All the Lutheran Ministers of the United States. 16°. Phil., Lutheran Pub. Soc., 1876. 85 cents.

History.

Hazelius, E. L. History of the American Lutheran Church from its Commencement in 1685 to 1842. 300 pp., 12°. Zanesville, O., E. C. Church, 1846.

Jacobs, H. E., *D. D.* History of the Evangelical Lutheran Church in the United States. 539 pp., 8°. N. Y.,

Christian Literature Co., 1893. (American Church History Series, v. 4.) $3.
> Includes a seven-page bibliography.

Jensson, J. C. American Lutheran Biographies. Milwaukee, Wis., 1891.

Lenker, *Rev.* J. N. Lutherans in All Lands. Ed. 4, enl. 841 pp., il., 8°. Milwaukee, Wis., Lutherans in All Lands Co., 1894. $2.75.
> Includes a one-page bibliography.

Sprague, W. B., *D. D.* Annals of the American Lutheran Pulpit. 216 pp., 8°. Phil., Lutheran Pub. Soc., 1869. $1. (Also forms part of v. 9 of Sprague's Annals.)

Wolf, E. J., *D. D.* Lutherans in America: a Story of Struggle, Progress, Influence and Marvellous Growth. 20+544 pp., 8°. N. Y., J. A. Hill & Co., 1890. $2.75.
> Includes a one-page bibliography.

Doctrines.

Augsburg Confession and Formula for the Government and Discipline of the Evangelical Lutheran Church in the United States. 71 pp., 16°. Phil., Lutheran Pub. Soc., 1890. 10 cents.

Holman, S. A., *ed.* Lectures on the Augsburg Confession: 21 Lectures by 21 Lecturers. 888 pp., 8°. Phil., Lutheran Pub. Soc., 1893. $3.

Loy, Matthias, *D. D.*, and others. Distinctive Doctrines and Usages of the Lutheran Church in the United States. 193 pp., 12°. Phil., Lutheran Pub. Soc., 1893. 75 cents.

Lutheran Church in the United States,—General Synod. Liturgy. 260 pp., 16°. Phil., Lutheran Pub. Soc. 75 cents.

Remensnyder, J. B., *D. D.* Lutheran Manual. N. Y., Boscher & Werfer, 1893.

Schmid, Heinrich, *D. D.* Doctrinal Theology of the Evangelical Lutheran Church; tr. by C. A. Hay and H. E. Jacobs. Ed. 2. 691 pp., 8°. Phil., Lutheran Pub. Soc., 1889. $4.

Periodicals.

The Lutheran, weekly. Phil. $2.25. Established 1861.

Lutheran Observer, weekly. Lancaster, Pa. $2. Established 1828.

Lutheran World, weekly. Cincinnati, O. $1. Established 1892.

Lutheran Quarterly. Gettysburg, Pa. $3. Established 1849.

Year-book.

Lutheran Almanac and Year-book for 1851–date. Il., 12°. Phil., Lutheran Pub. Soc. 10 cents.

MENNONITES.

History.

Cassel, D. K. History of the Mennonites. Phil., 1889.

Eby, B. Kurzgefasste Kirchengeschichte und Glaubenslehre der Taufgesinnten Christen oder Mennoniten. 16°. Elkhart, Ind., Mennonite Pub. Co., 1868. 75 cents.

Funk, J. F. The Mennonite Church and Her Accusers. Elkhart, Ind., Mennonite Pub. Co., 1878.

Horsch, John. The Mennonites: Their History, Faith and Practice. 40 pp., 12°. Elkhart, Ind., Mennonite Pub. Co., 1893. *Pamphlet.*
Includes a two-page bibliography.

Musser, Daniel. Reformed Mennonite Church : Its Rise and Progress with its Principles and Doctrines.

Ed. 2.   608 pp., 8°.   Lancaster, Pa., Inquirer Printing Co., 1878.

Doctrines.

Menno, Simon.   Complete Works ; tr. from the Dutch. Elkhart, Ind., Mennonite Pub. Co. $4.50.

Braght, T. J. van.   The Martyr's Mirror ; tr. from the Dutch by J. F. Funk and J. F. Sohm.   1093 pp., 8°. Elkhart, Ind., Mennonite Pub. Co., 1886. $5.

Catechism Presenting the Principles of the Mennonite Faith.   50 pp.   Elkhart, Ind., Mennonite Pub. Co.   10 cents.

Confession of Faith and Ministers' Manual.   Elkhart, Ind., Mennonite Pub. Co.   35 cents.

Periodicals.

Herald of Truth, a religious semi-monthly journal. Elkhart, Ind. $1.

Mennonitische Rundschau.   Elkhart, Ind.   75 cents.

Year-book.

Family Almanac for 1870–date.   8°.   Elkhart, Ind., Mennonite Pub. Co.

METHODISTS.

METHODIST EPISCOPAL CHURCH (NORTH).

(Including Methodism generally).

Bibliography.

Archibald, F. A., *D. D.*, *ed.*   Methodism and Literature : a Series of Articles on the Literary Enterprise and Achievements of the M. E. Church.   12°.   Cincinnati, Meth. Bk. Concern, 1883. $1.50.

Cavender, C. H.   Catalogue of Works in Refutation of Methodism from its Origin in 1729 to the Present, by H. C. Decanver, (pseud.).   Ed. 2.   8°.   N. Y., Author, 1868.

History.

Atkinson, *Rev.* John. Centennial History of American
Methodism. 559 pp., il., 8°. N. Y., Meth. Bk. Concern,
1884. $2.

Bangs, Nathan. History of the M. E. Church from
1766 to 1840. Ed. 3. 4 v., il., 12°. N. Y., Meth. Bk.
Concern, 1845. $3.60.

Buckley, J. M., *D. D.* History of the Methodists in
the United States. 8°. N. Y., Christian Literature Co.
(American Church History Series, v. 5). *Announced.*

Cooper, Ezekiel. Beams of Light on Early Methodism
in America. 12°. N. Y., Meth. Bk. Concern, 1887.
$1.25.

Curtiss, G. L., *D. D.* Manual of M. E. Church History. 8°. N. Y., Meth. Bk. Concern, 1893. $1.75.

Daniels, *Rev.* W. H. Illustrated History of Methodism
in Great Britain and America from the Wesleys to the
Present Time. 784 pp., il., 8°. N. Y., Meth. Bk. Concern, 1880.

Hyde, A. B. Story of Methodism. 12°. N. Y., M.
W. Hazen Co., 1889. $2.75.

McTyeire, H. N., *bp.* History of Methodism Down to
1884. 688 pp., 8°. Nashville, Tenn., M. E. Church,
South, Pub. House, 1884. $2.

Simpson, Matthew, *bp.* A Hundred Years of Methodism. 12°. N. Y., Meth. Bk. Concern, 1876. $1.75.

———Cyclopædia of Methodism Embracing Sketches
of its Rise, Progress and Present Conditions, with Biographical Sketches. New ed. 1031 pp., il., 4°. Phil.,
L. H. Everts, 1883.
Includes a sixteen-page bibliography.

Sprague, W. B., *D. D.* Annals of the American Pulpit :
Methodist. v. 7, 848 pp., por., 8°. N. Y., R. Carter &
Bros., 1865. $4.

Stevens, *Rev.* Abiel. History of the Religious Movement of the Eighteenth Century Called Methodism.   3 v., por., 12°. N. Y., Meth. Bk. Concern, 1858–61. $4.50.

————History of the M. E. Church in the United States of America.   4 v., por., 12°. N. Y., Meth. Bk. Concern, 1864–67. $10.

Tigert, J. J., *D. D.* Constitutional History of American Episcopal Methodism. 8°. Nashville, Tenn. Pub. House of the M. E. Church, South, 1895. $1.50.

Wood, E. M. Methodism and the Centennial of American Independence; with a Brief History of the Various Branches of Methodism.   412 pp., 12°. N. Y., Meth. Bk. Concern, 1876. 90 cents.

Doctrines and Polity.

Methodist Episcopal Church—General Conference of 1892. Doctrines and Discipline of the Church, 1892; ed. by Bishop [E. G.] Andrews.   352 pp., 16°. N. Y., Meth. Bk. Concern, 1892. 30 cents.

Merrill, S. M., *bp.* Digest of Methodist Law; or, Helps in the Administration of the Discipline of the M. E. Church. 218 pp., 16°. N. Y., Meth. Bk. Concern, 1885. 90 cents.

Neely, T. B., *D. D.* Evolution of Episcopacy and Organic Methodism. 12°. N. Y., Meth. Bk. Concern, 1888. $1.25.

————History of the Governing Conference in Methodism. 452 pp., 12°. Cincinnati, O., Meth. Bk. Concern, 1892. $1.50.

Pope, W. B., *D. D.* Compendium of Christian Theology: Analytical Outlines of a Course of Theological Study. Ed. 2, enl. 3 v., 8°. N. Y., Meth. Bk. Concern, 1881–82. $7.50.

Periodicals.

Central Christian Advocate, weekly. St. Louis, Meth. Bk. Concern. $2. Established 1860.

Christian Advocate, weekly. N. Y., Meth. Bk. Concern. $2.50. Established 1826.

Western Christian Advocate, weekly. Cincinnati, Meth. Bk. Concern. $2. Established 1834.

Zion's Herald, weekly. Bost., A. S. Weed. $2.50. Established 1823.

Methodist Review, bi-monthly. 8°. N. Y., Meth. Bk. Concern. $2.50. Established 1819.

NOTE.—T. L. Flood in the *Chautauquan* for Dec., 1894, has a good article on "Methodist Journalism," in which a good list of Methodist periodicals is given.

Year-books.

Methodist Year-book. 12°. N. Y., Meth. Bk. Concern 10 cents.

Methodist Episcopal Church—Annual Conference. Minutes, 1773-date. N. Y., Meth. Bk. Concern. $1 per volume for more recent ones in print.

——General Conference. Journal, 1796–1892. v. 1–12, 8°. N. Y., Meth. Bk. Concern. v. 1–3, $3 each; v. 4–5, $3.50 each; v. 6–12, $4 each.

Published quadrennially.

METHODIST EPISCOPAL CHURCH (SOUTH).

History.

Alexander, Gross, *D. D.* History of the Methodist Episcopal Church, South. 142 pp., 8°. N. Y., Christian Literature Co., 1894. $1. (Same is in American Church History Series, v. 11, pp. 1–142).

Includes a one-page bibliography.

Elliott, Charles, *D. D.* History of the Great Secession

from the Methodist Episcopal Church in 1845, Eventuating in the Organization of the M. E. Church, South. 1143 pp., 8°. Cincinnati, Swarmstedt & Poe, 1855. $2.50.

Merrill, S. M., *bp*. Organic Union of American Methodism. 112 pp., 12°. Cincinnati, Meth. Bk. Concern, 1892. 45 cents.

Discusses question of the reunion of M. E. Church, North and M. E. Church, South.

Myers, *Rev*. E. H. Disruption of the M. E. Church, 1844-46: comprising a 30 years' history of the relations of the two Methodisms. 12°. Nashville, Tenn., Pub. House of M. E. Church, South, 1875. $1.25.

Doctrines.

Hudson, H. T., *D. D.* Methodist Armor; or, A Popular Exposition of the Doctrines, Peculiar Usages and Ecclesiastical Machinery of the M. E. Church, South. 12°. Nashville, Tenn., Pub. House of M. E. Church, South. $1.

McTyeire, H. N., *bp*. Manual of the Discipline of the M. E. Church, South. 16°. Nashville, Tenn., Pub. House of M. E. Church, South. 60 cents.

Methodist Episcopal Church, South—General Conference. Discipline; ed. by W. P. Harrison, *D. D.* 24°. Nashville, Tenn., Pub. House of M. E. Church, South. 25 cents.

Peterson, P. A., *D. D.* History of the Revisions of the Discipline of the M. E. Church, South. 12°. Nashville, Tenn., Pub. House of M. E. Church, South, 1892. $1.

Periodicals.

Christian Advocate, weekly. Nashville, Tenn. $2.

Pacific Methodist Advocate, weekly. San Francisco. $2. Established 1891.

Methodist Review: a bi-monthly journal. 8°. Nashville, Tenn., Pub. House of M. E. Church, South. $2.

Year-books.

Methodist Episcopal Church, South—Annual Conference. Minutes, 1855–date. 8°. Nashville, Tenn., Pub. House of M. E. Church, South. 50 cents.

——General Conference. Journal, 1846–date. 8°. Nashville, Tenn., Pub. House of M. E. Church, South. 75 cents.

Published quadrennially.

FREE METHODISTS.

History.

Bowen, Elias, *D. D.* History of the Origin of the Free Methodist Church. North Chili, N. Y., Earnest Christian Pub. House. $1.25.

Terrill, *Rev.* J. G. Life of Rev. J. W. Redfield. Chicago, Free Methodist Pub. House. $1.25.

Doctrines and Polity.

Free Methodist Church. Doctrines and Discipline. Chicago, Free Meth. Pub. House, 1895. 35 cents.

Roberts, *Rev.* B. T. Why Another Sect? North Chili, N. Y., Earnest Christian Pub. House. $1.

Periodicals.

Free Methodist, weekly. Chicago, Free Meth. Pub. House.

Earnest Christian, a monthly magazine. North Chili, N. Y. $1.10. Established 1861.

Year-book.

Free Methodist Church. Annual Conference Record, Combined number. Chicago, Free Meth. Pub. House.

METHODIST PROTESTANTS.

Bassett, *Rev.* A. H.   Concise History of the Methodist Protestant Church from its Origin.   Ed. 3.   424 pp., 12°. Pittsburg, Pa., James Robinson, 1887.

Colhouer, *Rev.* T. H.   Sketches of the Founders of the Methodist Protestant Church and its Bibliography.   466 pp., 16°.   Pittsburg, Pa., Methodist Protestant Book Concern, 1880.

Includes a five-page bibliography.

Drinkhouse, E. J., *D. D.*   History of the Methodist Protestant Church.   3 v.   *Announced for publication in* 1896.

Paris, John, *D. D.*   History of the Methodist Protestant Church.   1849.

Williams, J. L.   History of the Methodist Protestant Church.   1843.

Doctines and Polity.

Colhouer, *Rev.* T. H.   Non-Episcopal Methodism.   1869.

Mayall, J. M.   Church Member's Manual.   1877.

Stephens, D. S., *D. D.*   Wesley and Episcopacy.

The foregoing works on this denomination can presumably be obtained from the Methodist Protestant Board of Publication, Pittsburg, Pa.

Periodicals.

Methodist Recorder.   Pittsburg, Pa.

Methodist Protestant.   Baltimore, Md.

MORAVIANS.

Bibliography.

Malin, W. G.   Catalogue of Books Relating to or Illustrating the History of the Unitas Fratrum or United Brethren, now generally known as the Moravian Church. Phil., 1881.

History.

Hamilton, J. T. History of the Unitas Fratrum or Moravian Church in the United States. 1895. (See American Church History Series, v. 8, pp. 425–508.)
Includes a three-page bibliography.

Reichel, *Rev.* L. T. Early History of the Church of the United Brethren in North America, 1734–48. Nazareth, Pa., 1888. (In Moravian Historical Society. Transactions. v. 3.)

Reichel, W. C. Memorials of the Moravian Church. v. 1, 366 pp., 8°. Phil., J. B. Lippincott Co., 1870. $3.50.

Schweinitz, Edmund de, *bp.* History of the Church Known as the Unitas Fratrum. Bethlehem, Pa., Moravian Publication Concern, 1885.
"Best for History up to 1722."

Thompson, A. C., *D. D.* Moravian Missions: Lectures. 12°. N. Y., Scribner's Sons, 1882. $2.
As the Moravians are essentially a missionary body, an account of their missions is included.

Doctrines.

Schweinitz, Edmund de, *bp.* Moravian Manual, Containing an Account of the Protestant Church of the Moravian United Brethren or Unitas Fratrum. Ed. 2 enl. 208 pp., 8°. Bethlehem, Pa., Moravian Publication Concern, 1869. $1.

Periodicals.

The Moravian, weekly. Bethlehem, Pa. $2. Established 1856.

Periodical Accounts Relating to Moravian Missions, quarterly. London, Eng., Moravian Publication Office, 32 Fetter Lane.

Year-book.

Moravian Almanack and Year-book. London, Eng., Moravian Publication Office.

MORMONS.

History.

Little, James. From Kirtland to Salt Lake City. 260 pp., il., 8°. Salt Lake City, Author, 1890. $1.50.

Historical Collateral.

Bancroft, H. H. History of Utah, 1540–1886. 47 + 808 pp., il., 8°. San Francisco, History Co., 1889. (Works v. 26.) $4.50.

Includes 26 pages of bibliography, of which a large number of the items relate to the Mormons.

Tullige, E. W. History of Salt Lake City. 896 + 172 + 36 pp., por., 8°. Salt Lake City, Star Printing Co., 1886.

Contains much valuable material.

Whitney, O. F. History of Utah. 4 v., pl., 8°. Salt Lake City, G. Q. Cannon & Sons Co. $30.

In progress: v. 1 and 2 so far published, 1895.

Doctrines.

Smith, Joseph, jr. Book of Mormon ; translated by Smith. Salt Lake City, G. Q. Cannon & Sons Co. $1 to $3.75.

First published at Palmyra, N. Y., in 1830.

——Book of Doctrine and Covenants of the Church of Jesus Christ of Latter-Day Saints. Salt Lake City, G. Q. Cannon & Sons Co. $1 to $3.75.

Ed. 3 published in N. Y., 1866.

Reynolds, George. Story of the "Book of Mormon." 494 pp., il., pl., 8°. Salt Lake City, Joseph Hyrum Parry, 1888. $2.50.

Penrose, C. W. "Mormon" Doctrine, Plain and, Sim-

ple ; or, Leaves from the Tree of Life. 69 pp., 12°.
Salt Lake City, G. Q. Cannon & Sons Co., 1882. 25 cents.
Richards, F. D., and Little, J. A. Compendium of the
Doctrines of the Gospel. Salt Lake City, G. Q. Cannon
& Sons Co. $1.
Published at Liverpool, Eng., 1857.

Periodical.

Deseret Weekly News, 15 June, 1850–date. Salt Lake
City. $2.50.
Also publish daily and semi-weekly editions.
Only books favorable to the Mormons are given, for the same
reason that only books favorable to Baptists, Lutherans, etc., are
included.

PRESBYTERIANS.

PRESBYTERIANS (NORTH).

(Including Presbyterians generally).

History.

Baird, *Rev.* S. J. History of the New School and of
the Questions Involved in the Disruption of the Presby-
terian Church in 1838. 12°. Phil., Claxton, Remsen &
Co., 1868. $2.
Blaikie, Alexander, *D. D.* History of Presbyterianism
in New England. 512 pp., 12°. Bost., A. Moore, 1881. $2.
Briggs, C. A., *D. D.* American Presbyterianism : Its
Origin and Early History. 373+142 pp., 8°. N. Y.,
Scribner's Sons, 1885. $3.
Gillette, E. H. History of the Presbyterian Church in
the United States. New ed. 2 v., 8°. Phil., Presbyterian
Bd. of Pub., 1873. $3.
Hays, G. P., *D. D.*, and others. Presbyterians : a Popu-
lar Narrative of their Origin, Progress, Doctrines and

Achievements.   544 pp., il., 8°.   N. Y., J. A. Hill & Co.,
1892. $2.75.

Hodge, Charles, *D. D.* Constitutional History of the
Presbyterian Church in the United States. Phil., Presbyterian Bd. of Publication, 1851. $1.

Nevin, Alfred, *D. D., ed.* Encyclopædia of the Pres-
byterian Church in the United States, Including the
Northern and Southern Assemblies. 1248 pp., il., 4°.
Phil., Presbyterian Encyclopædic Pub. Co., 1884. $10.

Presbyterian Reunion : a Memorial Volume, 1837–71.
568 pp., il., 8°.   N. Y., D. C. Lent & Co., 1871.

Sprague, W. B., *D. D.*   Annals of the American Pulpit :
Presbyterian. v. 3-4, por., 8°.   N. Y., R. Carter & Bros.,
1858. $8.

Thompson, R. E., *D. D.*   History of the Presbyterians
in the United States. 31+424 pp., 8°.   N. Y., Christian
Literature Co., 1895.   (American Church History Series,
v. 6.) $3.

Including bibliography, preface pp. 11-31.

Doctrines and Polity.

Bittinger, B. F., *D. D.* Manual of Law and Usages ;
Compiled from the Standards and Acts and Decisions of
the General Assembly of the Presbyterian Church. 170
pp., 16°.   Phil., Presbyterian Bd. of Pub., 1888.   75 cents.

McGill, A. T., *D. D.*   Church Government : a Treatise.
560 pp., 12°.   Phil., Presbyterian Bd. of Pub., 1888. $1.50.

Moore, W. E., *D. D.*   The Presbyterian Digest : a
Compend of the Acts and Deliverances of the General As-
sembly of the Presbyterian Church. New ed. 8°.   Phil.
Presbyterian Bd. of Pub., 1886. $2.

Presbyterian Church in the United States—General Assembly. Constitution of the Church, Containing the Confession of Faith, the Larger and Shorter Catechisms, the

Form of Government, the Book of Discipline and the Directory of Worship as Amended in 1892. 407 pp., 12°. Phil., Presbyterian Bd. of Pub., 1894. 60 cents.

Roberts, W. H., *D. D.* The Presbyterian System. 18°. Phil., Pres. Bd. of Pub., 1895. 50 cents.

Schaff, Philip, *D. D.* Creed Revision in the Presbyterian Churches. 67 pp., 8°. N. Y. Scribner's Sons, 1890. 50 cents (paper).

"Argument for revision."

Shedd, W. G. T., *D. D.* Proposed Revision of the Westminster Standards. 93 pp., 8°. N. Y., Scribner's Sons. 1890. 50 cents (paper).

"Argument against revision."

Smith, H. B., *D. D.* System of Christian Theology; edited by W. S. Karr., *D. D.* Ed. 4. 641 pp., 8°. N. Y., A. C. Armstrong & Son, 1890. $2.

Periodicals.

Church at Home and Abroad, published monthly. 8°. Phil., Presbyterian Bd. of Pub. $1. Established 1883.

Evangelist, weekly. N. Y. $3. Established 1870.

Interior, weekly. Chicago. $2.50. Established 1870.

Presbyterian, weekly. Phil., $2.65. Established 1831.

Presbyterian Banner, weekly. Pittsburg, $2.15. Established 1814.

Year-books.

Presbyterian Church in the United States—General Assembly. Minutes, 1789–date. 8°. Phil., Presbyterian Bd. of Pub. $1.50. (In paper at $1.)

————New School—General Assembly. Minutes, 1838–69. 8°. N. Y., Presbyterian Pub. Committee.

PRESBYTERIANS (SOUTH).

History.

Alexander, *Rev.* W. A., *ed.* Digest of the Acts of

the Presbyterian Church of the United States from its Re-
organization to the Assembly of 1887, with Historical and
Explanatory Notes.   560 pp., 8°.   Richmond, Va., Presbyterian Committee of Pub., 1888. $4.

Johnson, T. C., D. D.   History of the Southern Presbyterian Church, 1894.   (See American Church History
Series, v. 11, pp. 311–479.)

Includes a two-page bibliography.

Doctrines.

Presbyterian Church (South)—General Assembly.   Book
of Church Order, Adopted 1876.   Richmond, Va., Presbyterian Committee of Pub.   25 cents.

——Constitution of the Church, Confession of Faith,
the Larger and Shorter Catechisms, the form of Government, the Book of Discipline and the Directory of Worship as Ratified 1861.   Richmond, Va., Presbyterian Committee of Pub.   40 cents.

Periodicals.

Presbyterian Quarterly.   Richmond. $3.   Established
1887.

Central Presbyterian, weekly.   Richmond, Va. $2.50.
Established 1865.

Presbyterian, weekly, St. Louis. $2.50.   Established
1866.

Southwestern Presbyterian, weekly.   New Orleans. $2.
Established 1868.

"The church needs sadly a consolidation of some of its week-
lies."—*T. C. Johnson.*

Year-book.

Presbyterian   Church   (South)—General   Assembly.
Minutes, 1861–date.   8°.   Richmond, Va., Presbyterian
Committee of Pub.

CUMBERLAND PRESBYTERIANS.

History.

Beard, Richard, *D. D.* Biographical Sketches of the Early Ministers of the Cumberland Presbyterian Church. 2 v. Nashville, Tenn., Cumberland Presbyterian Pub. House, 1867.

Blake, T. C., *D. D.* Old Log House: History and Defense of the Cumberland Presbyterian Church. 293 pp., 18°. Nashville, Tenn., Cumberland Presbyterian Pub. House, 1878. 50 cents.

Foster, R. V., *D. D.* Sketch of the History of the Cumberland Presbyterian Church, 1894. (See American Church History Series, v. 11, pp. 257-309.)
Including a one-page bibliography.

Doctrines.

Cumberland Presbyterian Church—General Assembly. Confession of Faith. 286 pp. Nashville, Tenn., Cumberland Presbyterian Pub. House, 1875. 40 cents.

Crisman, E. B., *D. D.* Origin and Doctrines of the Cumberland Presbyterian Church. 55+150 pp., 12°. Nashville, Tenn., Cumberland Presbyterian Pub. House, 1877. 40 cents.

Howard, J. M., *D. D.* Creed and Constitution of the Cumberland Presbyterian Church, 1885.

Miller, A. B., *D. D.* Doctrines and Genius of the Cumberland Presbyterian Church. 320 pp., 8°. Nashville, Tenn., Cumberland Presbyterian Pub. House, 1892. $1.50.
" A fair statement of the doctrines."—*R. V. Foster.*

Periodicals.

Cumberland Presbyterian, weekly. Nashville, Tenn. $2. Established 1841.
" Official organ of the Church."

Observer, weekly. St. Louis, D. M. & C. M. Harris.
$1.50. Established 1877.

Year book.

Cumberland Presbyterian Church—General Assembly.
Minutes, 1831–date. 8°. Nashville, Tenn., Cumberland
Presbyterian Pub. House.

REFORMED PRESBYTERIANS.

History.

Glasgow, *Rev.* W. M. History of the Reformed Presbyterian Church in America. 892 pp., il. Baltimore,
Md., Hill & Harvey, 1888. $2.50.

McFeeters, J. C. Covenanters in America. 235 pp.
Phil.. Spangler & Davis, 1892.

Spague, W. B., *D. D.* Annals of the American Pulpit: Reformed Presbyterian. 89 pp., 8°. 1869. (In his
Annals, v. 9.)

Doctrines.

Foster, *Rev.* J. M. Reformation Principles: Stated
and Applied. 448 pp., 12°. N. Y., F. H. Revell, 1890.
$1.50.

McAllister, D., *D. D.* Manual of Christian Civil Government. 313 pp. Phil., Aldine Press, 1890.

Periodicals.

Christian Nation, weekly. N. Y. $1.50. Established
1894.

Christian Statesman, weekly. Pittsburg. $2. Estab-
lished 1867.

Reformed Presbyterian and Covenanter, monthly. 12°.
Pittsburg. $1. Established 1867.

The minutes of the synod of the church are regularly published
in its columns.

UNITED PRESBYTERIANS.

History.

Harper, R. D., *D. D.* The Church Memorial. 407 pp., 12°. Xenia, O.
"Gives an account of the proceedings which resulted in the formation of the church."

Scouller, J. B., *D. D.* History of the United Presbyterian Church of North America, 1894. (See American Church History Series, v. 11, pp. 143-225.)

———Manual of the United Presbyterian Church of North America. 788 pp., 8°. Pittsburg, Pa., United Presbyterian Bd. of Pub., 1888. $2. (Ed. 2, 1892 ?)

United Presbyterian Church—General Assembly. Digest of the General Assembly, 1859-78. Pittsburg, Pa., United Presbyterian Bd. of Pub., 1879. (Later edition including 1891 ?)

Doctrines.

Reid, W. J., *D. D.* United Presbyterianism. 12°. Pittsburg, Pa., United Presbyterian Bd. of Pub., 1882. $1.

Periodicals.

Christian Instructor and United Presbyterian Witness, weekly. Phil., Collins & Co. $2. Established 1846.

Midland, weekly. Chicago and Omaha, Neb. $2. Established 1884.

United Presbyterian, weekly. Pittsburg, Pa., H. J. Murdoch & Co. $2. Established 1842.

Year-book.

United Presbyterian Church—General Assembly. Minutes. 8°. Pittsburg, Pa., United Presbyterian Bd. of Pub. 30 cents.

REFORMED CHURCHES.
REFORMED (DUTCH) CHURCH.
History.

Brinkerhoff, Jacob. History of the True Reformed Dutch Church in the United States. 12°. N. Y., Reformed Church Bd. of Pub., 1873. 75 cents.

Corwin, E. T., *D. D.* History of the Reformed Church, Dutch. 1895. (See American Church History Series. v. 8, pp. 1–212.)

Includes a five-page bibliography.

———Manual of the Reformed Church in America (formerly Reformed Protestant Dutch Church), 1628–1878. Ed. 2 enl. 676 pp., il., 8°. N. Y., Bd. of Pub. of Reformed Church, 1879.

Includes lists of all books written by Reformed Dutch clergymen.

Demarest, D. D., *D. D.* Reformed Church in America: its Origin, Development and Characteristics. 210 pp., 8°. N. Y., Bd. of Pub. of Reformed Church, 1889. $1.60.

Reformed (Dutch) Church in America—General Synod. Centennial Discourses: a Series of [22] Sermons Delivered in 1876. Ed. 2. 601 pp., 8°. N. Y., Bd. of Pub. of Reformed Church, 1877. $3.

Sprague, W. B., *D. D.* Annals of American Reformed Dutch Pulpit. 242 pp., 8°. N. Y., Bd. of Pub. of Reformed Church, 1869. $1.50. (Also forms part of v. 9 of his Annals.)

Van Pelt, *Rev.* Daniel. Chronological Table of Events in the History of the Reformed Dutch Church in America. 8°. N. Y., Bd. of Pub. of Reformed Church. 50 cents.

Doctrines.

Reformed (Dutch) Church—General Synod. Constitu-

tion. 354 pp., 16°. N. Y., William Dunrell, 1793. (Many
modern editions to be bought at Bd. of Pub. of Reformed
Church, New York.)

"This contains the standards of doctrine (creeds and confessions), liturgy and rules of church government."—*E. T. Corwin.*

Bethune, G. W., *D. D.* Expository Lectures on the
Heidelberg Catechism. 2 v., 8°. N. Y., Sheldon & Co.,
1864. $4.50.

Birdsall, *Rev.* Edward. Church Member's Manual: a
Hand-book for the Members of the Reformed (Dutch)
Church. N. Y., Bd. of Pub. of Reformed Church, 1894.
30 cents.

Text and translations of the Belgic confession, Heidelberg catechism and Canons of the Synod of Dort may be
found in Schaff's Creeds of Christendom.

See also Reformed (German) Church: Doctrines.

Periodicals.

Christian Intelligencer, weekly. N. Y. $2.65. Es-
tablished 1829.

De Hope, weekly. Holland, Mich. $2. Established
1866.

In the Dutch language.

Year-book.

Reformed (Dutch) Church in America—General Synod.
Acts and Proceedings, 1794–date. 8°. N. Y., Bd. of Pub.
of Reformed Church. 65 cents a year.

———Acts and Proceedings, 1738–1812. v. 1, 8°. N.
Y., Bd. of Pub. of Reformed Church, 1859. $1.50 (pa-
per).

This volume reprinted from the original documents: mostly
translated from the Dutch.

REFORMED (GERMAN) CHURCH IN THE UNITED STATES.

Bibliography.

Fisher, C. G., *D. D.*   History of Publication Efforts in the Reformed Church.   Phil., Reformed Church Pub. House, 1885.

History.

Dubbs, J. H., *D. D.*   History of the Reformed Church, German.   1895.   (See American Church History Series, v. 8, pp. 213–423.)
Includes a seven-page bibliography.
————Historic Manual of the Reformed Church in the United States.   433 pp., 8°.   Lancaster, Pa., Author, 1885. $2.

Swander, J. I.   The Reformed Church.   Dayton, O., 1889.

Doctrines.

Heidelberg Catechism in German, Latin and English, with an Historical Introduction; Prepared and Published by the German Reformed Church.   Tercentenary ed. 277 pp., sq. 8°.   N. Y., Charles Scribner's Sons, 1863. $3.50.

Reformed (German) Church in the United States.   Liturgy ; or, Order of Christian Worship for the Church. 367 pp., 8°.   Phil., S. R. Fisher & Co., 1867.

Gerhart, E. V., *D. D.*   Institutes of the Christian Religion.   2 v., 8°.   N. Y., Funk & Wagnalls Co., 1894. $6.

Russell, G. B., *D. D.*   Creeds and Customs: a Popular Hand-book Treating of the Doctrines and Practices of the Reformed Church.   12°.   Phil., Reformed Church Pub. House, 1869. $1.50.

Periodicals.

Reformed Quarterly Review. 8°. Phil., Reformed Church Pub. House. $3.
Continuation of Mercersburg Review, established 1849.
Christian World, weekly. Dayton, O. $2. Established 1846.
Reformed Church Messenger, weekly. Phil., Reformed Church Pub. House. $2. Established 1832.
Die Reformirte Kirchenzeitung, weekly. Cleveland, O., L. Praikschatis. Established 1838.

Year-book.

Almanac for the Reformed Church in the United States for the Year 1864–date. 8°. Phil., Reformed Church Pub. House. 12 cents.

ROMAN CATHOLICS.

As this church lays claim to and aims at catholicity, the church of one country is organically connected with the other members of the world church. Hence a list which is confined, as mine is, to the church in this country, is rather inadequate. To supply this deficiency my friend, Father McMahon, has at my request furnished a more representative list of the world literature of the Catholic Church. This list is given in the appendix. Although our lists duplicate each other in a few instances, yet his list should be regarded as supplemental to my own.

Bibliography.

Finnotti, *Rev.* J. M. Bibliographia Catholica Americana : a List of Works by Catholic Authors and publishers in the United States, 1784–[1825]. 318 pp., 8°. N. Y., Catholic Publication Society, 1872. $5.
May be bought now for $2

Hughes, *Rev.* Thomas, and others. The Library of a Priest: [a series of articles]. 1895. (See American Ecclesiastical Review, v. 12, pp. 1–13, 138–50, 226–45, 382–88; v. 13, pp. 1–38, 45–47.)

Catholic Book News, [six times a year]. 8⁰. N. Y., Benziger Bros. *Free.*

Good to keep track of current Catholic books.

History.

Addis, W. B. and Arnold, Thomas. Catholic Dictionary : Containing Some Account of the Doctrines, Discipline, Rites, Ceremonies, Councils, and Religious Orders of the Catholic Church. Ed. 6 enl. 958 pp., 8⁰. N. Y., Catholic Pub. Soc., 1889. $5.

Businger, *Rev.* L. C. Christ in His Church : a Catholic Church History ; trans. by Richard Brennan. [also] History of the Church in America, by J. G. Shea. 426 pp., il., 8⁰. N. Y., Benziger Bros., 1881. $2.

Le Clercq, Chrestien, *Père.* First Establishment of the Faith in New France ; trans. with notes by J. G. Shea. 2 v., pors. and fac-sims., 8⁰. N. Y., J. G. Shea, 1881.

Original first published in 1691.

Murray, J. O. Popular History of the Catholic Church in the United States. Ed. 3. 619 pp., 8⁰. N. Y., D. & J. Sadlier & Co., 1876. $3.50.

O'Gorman, Thomas., *D. D.* History of the Roman Catholic Church in the United States. 8⁰. N. Y., Christian Literature Co., 1895. $3. (American Church History Series, v. 9.)

Shea, J. D. G. Hierarchy of the Catholic Church in the United States, Embracing Sketches of All the Archbishops and Bishops . . . an Account of the Plenary Councils, . . . and a Brief History of the Church in the United States. 402 pp., 8⁰. N. Y., Catholic Pub. Soc., 1886.

Shea, J. D. G. History of the Catholic Church Within the Limits of the United States, from the First Attempted Colonization to the Present Time. 4 v., il., 4°. N. Y. J. G. Shea, 1886–92. $20. (To be had of Catholic Pub· Soc., N. Y.)

Contents.

v. 1. Catholic Church in colonial days, 1521–1763.

v. 2. Life and times of John Carroll, a history of the Catholic Church, 1763–1815.

v. 3. History of Catholic Church, 1808–43.

v. 4. "   "   "   "   1843–66.

(2d Plenary Council of Baltimore).

Never completed : the great standard history.

——History of the Catholic Missions Among the Indians of the United States, 1529–1854. 514 pp., il., 12°. N. Y., P. J. Kenedy, 1855. $2.50.

World's Columbian Catholic Congress, 1893. 202 pp., 8°. Chic., J. S. Hyland & Co., 1893.

Published in connection with a history of the Catholic educational exhibit, etc., and an epitome of Catholic church progress in the United States. Total pp., 713.

Doctrines.

Catholic Church—Third Plenary Council of Baltimore. Manual of Prayers for the Use of the Catholic Laity. 792 pp., 24°. Balt., John Murphy & Co., 1889. $1.25.

Gibbons, James, *Card.* The Faith of Our Fathers. Ed. 36. 438 pp., 16°. Balt., John Murphy & Co., 1890. $1.

Hunter, *Rev.* S. J. Outlines of Dogmatic Theology. 3 v. N. Y., Benziger Bros., 1895. $1.50 each.

Only vols. 1 and 2 so far published.

Searle, *Rev.* G. M. Plain Facts for Fair Minds : an Appeal to Candor and Common-Sense. 360 pp., N. Y., Catholic Book Exchange, 1895. 10 cents.

Smith, S. B., *D. D.* Elements of Ecclesiastical Law :

Compiled with Reference to the Latest Decisions of the
Sacred Congregation of Cardinals. New ed., enl. 3 v., 8°.
N. Y., Benziger Bros., 1893. $7.50.

Contents.

v. 1. Ecclesiastical persons.
v. 2.   "   trials.
v. 3.   "   punishments.

Periodicals.

American Catholic Quarterly Review, 1876–date. 8°.
Phil., Hardy & Mahony. $5.
American Ecclesiastical Review ; a monthly for the
clergy, 1889–date. 8°. Phil. $3.50.
Catholic World, monthly, 1865–date. 8°. N. Y., Co-
lumbus Press. $3.
Catholic Review, weekly. N. Y., P. V. Hickey. $3.
Established 1871.
Catholic Standard, weekly. Phil., C. A. Hardy. $2.50.
Established 1865.
Church Progress and Catholic World, weekly. St. Louis,
Catholic Pub. Co. $1.50   Established 1877.
The Republic, weekly, Bost. $2.50.   Established 1881.

Year-books.

Hoffman's Catholic Directory, Almanac and Clergy List.
Milwaukee, Hoffman Bros. Co.   50 cents a year.
Illustrated Catholic Family Annual, 1869–date.   12°.
N. Y., Catholic School Book Co.   10 cents.
Sadlier's Catholic Directory, Almanac and Ordo, for
1864–date. v. 32–date.   12°. N. Y., D. & J. Sadlier &
Co. $1.50.
First published in 1833 with title "United States Catholic Al-
manac."

SALVATION ARMY.

"Although the Army is not a church in the accepted
phraseology (that is, people who administer sacraments,
etc.), yet it is a church in the same sense as the Society
of Friends is a church." The foregoing statement was
furnished in a personal letter from one of the officers of
the Army. The following list was, in part, furnished
by another officer. It includes some books which deal
more specifically with the same work in England.

General Works.

Booth, *Mrs.* Ballington. Wanted, Antiseptic Christians.
————Beneath Two Flags. 12°. N. Y., Funk & Wag-
nalls, 1889. $1.
————New York's Inferno. 25 cents.
Booth, *General* William. In Darkest England, and the
Way Out. 300 pp., 12°. N. Y., Funk & Wagnalls, 1890.
$1.
————Salvation Soldiery, 1882.
————Training of Children, 1884.
Booth, *Mrs.* William. Aggressive Christianity, 1881.
————Popular Christianity, 1882.
————Salvation Army in Relation to the Church and
State, 1883. 25 cents.

Periodicals.

The War Cry, weekly. N. Y. $2.
The Conqueror, monthly. 1892–date. N. Y. $1.
The national headquarters of the Salvation Army are 120-24
W. 14th St., New York, where any Salvation Army literature can
be obtained.

SHAKERS.

History.

Evans, F. W. Shakers : Compendium of the Origin,

History, Principles, Rules and Regulations, Government and Doctrines of the United Society of Believers in Christ's Second Appearing. 184 pp., 16°. N. Y., Appleton & Co., 1859. 75 cents.

Green, Calvin and Wells, S. T. Summary View of the Millennial Church or United Society of Believers Commonly Called Shakers. Ed. 2 enl. 384 pp., 12°. Albany, C. Van Benthuysen, 1848.

Robinson, C. E. Concise History of the United Society of Believers Called Shakers. 134 pp., il. 8°. East Canterbury, N. H., H. C. Blinn, 1893. 75 cents.

Doctrines.

Eads, H. L. Shaker Sermons, Scripto-rational, Containing the Substance of Shaker Theology. New ed. enl. 320 pp., 8°. East Canterbury, N. H., H. C. Blinn. $1.25.
Ed. 3 was published 1884. This is probably ed. 4.

Periodicals.

The Manifesto, a monthly periodical. East Canterbury. N. H. 75 cents.
Note.—Almost any Shaker publication now in print may be obtained from H. C. Blinn, East Canterbury, N. H.

SWEDENBORGIANS.

History.

Field, *Rev.* G. Memoirs, Incidents and Reminiscences of the Early History of the New Church in Michigan, Indiana, Illinois and Adjacent States, and Canada. 368 pp., 12°. N. Y., 1879. Bost., Mass. New Church Union. $1.

Hindmarsh, Robert. Rise and Progress of the New Jerusalem Church in England and other Parts. 460 pp., 8°. Lond., Hodson & Son, 1861. Bost., Mass. New Church Union. $1.25.

New Jerusalem—General Convention. Reprint of the Early Journals, 1817–35. 3 v., 8°. Bost., Mass. New Church Union. $1.50.

Doctrines.

Swedenborg, Emanuel. The Four Leading Doctrines of the New Church, Concerning the Lord, the Sacred Scriptures, Faith and Life. 247 pp., 8°. N. Y., American Swedenborg Printing & Pub. Co., 1873. 75 cents.

——Liturgy for the New Church. 16°. Bost., Mass. New Church Union. $1,25.

——The True Christian Religion : the Universal Theology of the New Church. 613 pp., 8°. Phil., J. B. Lippincott Co., 1872. $1.50.

Parsons, Theophilus. Outlines of the Religion and Philosophy of Swedenborg. New ed. 318 pp., 16°. Bost., Mass. New Church Union, 1894. 75 cents.

Swift, Edmund, jr. Manual of the Doctrines of the New Church. 16°. Bost., Mass. New Church Union. 40 cents.

Periodicals.

New Church Review, quarterly. Jan., 1894–date. 8°. Bost., Mass. New Church Union. $2.

New Church Messenger, weekly. N. Y. and Orange, N. J., New Church Bd. of Pub. $3. Established 1855.

Year-books.

New Jerusalem—General Convention. Journal of the Annual Session, 1821–date. 8°. Bost., Mass. New Church Union.

New Church Almanac for 1889. 164 pp., il. por., 12°. Bost., Mass. New Church Union.

Publication not continued. However, it claims to " contain the best historical account to be had of the New Jerusalem Church."

UNITARIANS.

Bibliography.

Gillett, E. H., *comp.*   Bibliography of the Unitarian Controversy.   (See Historical Magazine, v. 19, pp. 316–24, Apr., 1871.)

History.

Allen, J. H., *D. D.*   Historical Sketch of the Unitarian Movement Since the Reformation.   249 pp., 8⁰.   N. Y., Christian Literature Co., 1894. $1.50.   (Also see American Church History Series, v. 10, pp. 1–249.)

———Our Liberal Movement in Theology, Shown in the History of Unitarianism in New England.   220 pp., 16⁰.   Bost., Roberts Bros., 1882. $1.25.

Frothingham, O. B.   Boston Unitarianism, 1820–50: a Study of the Life and Works of Nathaniel Langdon Frothingham.   272 pp., 8⁰.   N. Y., G. P. Putnam's Sons, 1890. $1.75.

Sprague, W. B., *D. D.*   Annals of the American Pulpit: Unitarian Congregational.   v. 8, 578 pp., por., 8⁰. N. Y., R. Carter & Bros., 1865. $4.

Unitarianism, Its Origin and History: a Course of Sixteen Lectures Delivered in Channing Hall, Boston, 1888–89.   29+394 pp., 12⁰.   Bost., American Unitarian Association, 1890. $1.

Doctrines.

Chadwick, *Rev.* J. W.   Old and New Unitarian Belief. 246 pp., por., 8⁰.   Bost., G. H. Ellis, 1894. $1.50.

Clarke, J. F., and others.   Modern Unitarianism.   218 pp., 12⁰.   Phil., J. B. Lippincott Co., 1886. $1.25.

Ellis, G. E.   Half-century of the Unitarian Controversy with Particular Reference to its Origin, its Course and its

Prominent Subjects Among the Congregationalists of Massachusetts. 511 pp., 8°. Bost., Crosby, Nichols & Co., 1857. $1.50.

Farley, F. A., *D. D.* Unitarianism Defined: the Scripture Doctrine of the Father, Son and Holy Ghost. Ed. 2. 272 pp., 12°. Bost., American Unitarian Association, 1873. 60 cents.

Periodicals.

Christian Register, weekly. Bost., $3. Established 1821.

Pacific Unitarian, monthly. San Francisco. $1. Established 1892.

Unitarian, monthly. Bost. and Ann Arbor, Mich. $1.

Unity, weekly. Chic. $1. Established 1878.

Year-books.

Year-book of the Unitarian Congregational Churches. 12°. Bost., American Unitarian Association. 20 cents.

American Unitarian Association. Anniversary, with the Annual Report of the Board of Directors, 1826–date. 12°. Bost., American Unitarian Association.

UNITED BRETHREN IN CHRIST.

Bibliography.

Shuey, W. A. Manual of the United Brethren Publishing House: Historical and Descriptive. 20 + 371 pp., il., 12°. Dayton, O., United Brethren Pub. House, 1893. $1.50.

History.

Berger, D., *D. D.* History of the Church of the United Brethren in Christ. 1894. (See American Church History Series, v. 12, pp. 309-82.)

Includes a five-page bibliography.

Lawrence, John.   History of the Church of the United
Brethren in Christ.   2 v. in 1, 12°.   Dayton, O., United
Brethren Pub. House, 1890–93. $2.50.

Doctrines.

Shuey, E. L.   Handbook of the United Brethren in
Christ.   New ed. enl.   78 pp., 16°.   Dayton, O., United
Brethren Pub. House, 1893.   15 cents.

Weaver, Jonathan, *bp.*, *ed.*   Christian Doctrines: a
Comprehensive View of Doctrinal and Practical Theology
by Thirty-seven Writers.   611 pp., 8°.   Dayton, O.,
United Brethren Pub. House, 1894. $2.25.

United Brethren in Christ.   Origin, Doctrine, Constitution and Discipline.   224 pp., 16°.   Dayton, O., United
Brethren Pub. House, 1893.   25 cents.

Periodicals.

Religious Telescope, weekly.   Dayton, O., United
Brethren Pub. House. $2.   Established 1834.

Quarterly Review of the United Brethren in Christ.
1890–date.   8°.   Dayton, O., United Brethren Pub.
House. $1.50.

Year-books.

Year-book of the United Brethren in Christ, 1867–date.
12°.   Dayton, O., United Brethren Pub. House.   10
cents.

United Brethren in Christ.   Official Report of the De-
bates and Proceedings of the General Conference, 1873–
date.   Dayton, O., United Brethren Pub. House.   75
cents each (except for 1893, $1).

Quadrennial.

UNIVERSALISTS.

Bibliography.

Eddy, Richard, *D. D., comp.*. Universalism in America. 1884–86. v. 2., pp. 485–599.

Contains 2,278 titles.

History.

Eddy, Richard, *D. D.* History of Universalism. 1894. (See American Church History Series, v. 10., pp. 251–493.)

Includes a two-page bibliography.

———Universalism in America: a History, 1636–1886. 2 v., 8°. Bost., Universalist Pub. House, 1884–86. $3.50.

Thomas, A. C. A Century of Universalism in Philadelphia and New York. 350 pp., 12°. Bost., Universalist Pub. House, 1872.

"Of more than local interest."

Doctrines.

Adams, J. G., *D. D.* Fifty Notable Years: Views of the Ministry of Christian Universalism During the Last Half Century. 336 pp., 15 por., 12°. Bost., Universalist Pub. House, 1882. $1.20.

Hanson, J. W., *D. D.* 'Διών–α'ιώνιος: Excursus on the Greek Word Rendered Everlasting, Eternal, in the Holy Bible Shown to Denote Limited Duration. 174 pp., 12°. Bost., Universalist Pub. House, 1889. 75 cents.

Latest Word of Universalism: Thirteen Essays by Thirteen Clergymen. 295 pp., 16°. Bost., Universalist Pub. House, 1878. 75 cents.

Thayer, T. B., *D. D.* Origin and History of the Doctrine of Endless Punishment. New ed. enl. 280 pp., 12°. Bost., 1881.

———Theology of Universalism: Being a Scripture Exhibition of its Doctrines and Teachings and Their Logical Connections and Moral Relations.   432 pp., 12°. Bost., Universalist Pub. House, 1862. $1.

Periodicals.

Christian Leader, weekly.   Bost., Universalist Pub. House. $2.50.   Established 1819.

Gospel Banner, weekly.   Augusta, Me., B. A. Mead & Co. $2.   Established 1835.

Universalist, weekly.   Chic., Universalist Pub. House. $2.50.   Established 1828.

Year-book.

Universalist Register, 1836–date.   16°.   Bost., Universalist Pub. House.   25 cents.

APPENDIX.

A List of the Most Important Catholic Works of the World.

Compiled by

REV. JOSEPH H. McMAHON.

APPENDIX.

ROMAN CATHOLIC BIBLIOGRAPHY.

Year-books.

I. *Gerarchia Cattolica.* Roma. Tipografia Vaticana. Contains the official list of the entire Hierarchy of the Roman Catholic Church throughout the world, *i. e.*, Pope, Cardinals, Bishops and Prelates, together with the names of sees, residential or titular, the membership of the Roman Congregations, etc.

II. Hoffman's Catholic Directory. Hoffman Brothers, Milwaukee, Wis. While unofficial, a reliable guide to the Bishops, Priests, religious communities and ecclesiastical institutions of the Roman Catholic Church in the United States. The *Clergy List Quarterly* is a directory of ecclesiastics issued quarterly in connection with above, and giving changes of address, etc., necrology, etc. Chic. and Cin.

III. Sadlier's Catholic Directory. D. & J. Sadlier, New York, is also an unofficial directory, somewhat differently arranged from the above.

IV. Reports of Diocesan School Boards. Each diocese has a board which supervises the system of parochial schools.

V. Parish Monthly Calendars. Many parishes in various dioceses issue calendars which contain items of parochial interest.

VI. Catholic Family Annual. Catholic School Book Co., N. Y.

VII. Catholic Home and Family Almanac. Benziger Brothers, N. Y.

PERIODICAL LITERATURE.

NOTE.—This list embraces only the principal periodicals in the U. S. A complete list is given in Hoffman's Catholic Directory.

Quarterlies.

The American Catholic Quarterly Review. Phil. Archbishop Ryan, Editor.

The Catholic University Bulletin. Catholic University, Washington, D. C. Rev. T. J. Shahan, *D. D.*, Editor.

The United States Catholic Historical Magazine. Published by the United States Catholic Historical Society of N. Y.

The American Catholic Historical Record. Published by the Catholic Historical Society of Philadelphia.

Monthlies.

The Catholic World. Illustrated magazine of general literature. Published by the Paulist Fathers, N. Y.

The Month. An American edition of a notable English magazine. John Murphy Co., Baltimore, Md.

The Messenger of the Sacred Heart. An illustrated magazine published by the Jesuit Fathers as the official organ of the League of the Sacred Heart, New York.

The Pilgrim of our Lady of Martyrs: a supplementary monthly issue of the Messenger.

Donahoe's Magazine. An illustrated magazine devoted to general Catholic interests and literature. Boston. Published by the Donahoe Magazine Co.

The Rosary, an illustrated magazine published by the Dominican Fathers in the interests of the Confraternity of the Rosary, Rev. J. L. O'Neil, O. P., Editor, N. Y.

The American Ecclesiastical Review. A monthly publication for the Roman Catholic clergy: treats theological and liturgical subjects, contains official documents from **Rome.** Rev. H. J. Heuser, Editor, St. Charles Seminary, Overbrook, Pa. Publication Office, New York.

The Seminary, an illustrated high class monthly periodical issued in the interests of St. Joseph's Seminary, N. Y. John Mulally, Esq., Editor.

The Catholic Reading Circle Review, the official organ of the Catholic Summer School of America, and of the Catholic Reading Circle Union. Youngstown, O., Warren E. Mosher, Editor.

Weeklies.

The principal Catholic weekly papers are:

The Catholic Review, of New York.

The Catholic News, of New York.

The Freeman's Journal, of New York.

The Pilot, of Boston.

The Republic, of Boston.

The Sacred Heart Review, of Cambridge.

The New World, of Chicago.

Church Progress, of St. Louis.

The Catholic Standard and Times, of Philadelphia.

The Church News, of Washington, D. C.

The Catholic Mirror, of Baltimore.

The Citizen, of Milwaukee.

The Colorado Catholic, of Denver.

The Monitor, of San Francisco.

BIBLIOGRAPHY ROMAN CATHOLIC CHURCH.*

[NOTE:—For those who desire a bibliography as complete as possible, Nomenclator Literarius Recentioris Theologiæ Catholicæ Theologos exhibens qui inde a Concilio Tridentino floruerunt, H. Hurter, S. J., 2d Ed. 3 vols., Innsbruck, 1892, will be found invaluable.]

* Adapted principally from a series of articles in The American Ecclesiastical Review.

I. WORKS ON DOGMATIC THEOLOGY IN GENERAL.

S. Thomæ Aquinatis, O. P.   (†1274). *Opera Omnia.*
(Various editions : Rome, 1572, 17 vols.; Paris, 1660, 23
vols.; Venice, 1787, 28 vols.; Parma, 1852–71, 25 vols.;
Paris, 1871–80, 34 vols.;—a splendid folio edition is just
now being published in Rome, seven volumes having al-
ready been issued under the patronage of Pope Leo.)

Summa Theologica, the crowning work of his life, is
the best synthesis of Catholic Doctrine hitherto framed.

Quæstiones Disputatæ, in which some of the deepest
problems of Theology are more fully explained than in
the *Summa Theologica.*

S. Bonaventuræ, O.S.F. (†1274). *Opera Omnia.* (Rome,
1588-96; Lyons, 1668; Paris, 1864–71; the best edition is
in course of publication at Quaracchi.   Six volumes have
thus far appeared.)

His best works are: *In Quatuor Sententiarum libros Ex-
positio,* a complete course of dogmatic theology, considered to be one of the best commentaries on the famous
Sentences of Peter the Lombard ; his *Opuscula,* particularly *Breviloquium, De Reductione Artium ad Theologiam, Itin-
erarium Mentis ad Deum.*

Melchioris Cani, O.P. (†1560).   *De locis Theologicis libri 12* (Salamanca, 1563; Venice, 1567; Louvain, 1569;
Lyons, 1704; inserted in Migne's Theol. Curs. Completus,
vol. 2).   This is beyond doubt the classical work on the
important subject it deals with.

F. Suarez, S. J. (†1617). *Opera Omnia.* (Lyons, 1630;
Venice, 1740–57; Paris, 1856).

His works are the most complete and exhaustive exposition of scholastic theology.   Those too busy to read
his twenty-four Folios will peruse with great profit the
summary of the same, published by F. Noël, S.J., (1729)

and reprinted by Migne, *Theologiæ R. P. F. Suarez Summa seu Compendium;* or the *Summa theologiæ scholasticæ* written by *Martinus Becanus, S.J.* (Mainz, 1612; Rouen, 1657). Collegii Salmanticensis Cursus Theologicus (Lyons, 1679; Paris, 1870). This is a commentary on St. Thomas' *Summa Theologica,* written by three Carmelites, *Antonius a Matre Dei, Dominicus a S. Teresia* and *Joannes ab Annuntiatione.* Deep, clear, concise and yet exhaustive, it is considered by many to be the best exposition and defence of Thomistic theology.

Petavii, S. J. (†1652). *Dogmata Theologica.* (Paris, 1644–50; Amsterdam, 1700; Venice, 1757; Rome, 1857; Paris, 1865). This is the best *patristic* theology published.

L. Thomassini (†1695). *Dogmata Theologica* (Paris, 1680; Venice, 1730; Paris, 1864). His erudition is prodigious, his style clear and eloquent, though somewhat diffuse.

L. Lessii, S.J. (†1623). *De Perfectionibus Moribusque Divinis* (Antwerp, 1620; Paris, 1620; Lyons, 1656; Freiburg, 1861; Paris, 1881). A treatise on the Divine Attributes, and on God's Providence.

Martinez de Ripalda, S. J. (†1648). *De Ente Supernaturali* (Bordeaux, 1635; Lyons, 1645, 1663; Paris, 1870). The most exhaustive treatise on the supernatural order, grace, infused virtues, etc.

A. Arnauld (†1694); P. Nicolle (†1695); E. Renaudot (†1720). *Traité de l'Eucharistie, La Perpétuité de la Foi de l'Eglise catholique touchant l'Eucharistie* (Paris, 1664, 1669, 1713, 1841). An historical work containing all the documents, ancient and modern, Greek and Latin, on the dogma of the Blessed Eucharist, and, incidentally, on the other sacraments.

J. Morin (†1659). *Commentarius Historicus de Disciplina in Administratione Sacr. Pœnitentiæ* (Paris, 1651; Venice, 1702). A work of remarkable erudition.

Chardon, O.S.B. (†1771). *Histoire des Sacrements* (Paris, 1745; Theol. Curs. Completus, vol. 20).

Billuart, O.P. (†1757). *Summa S. Thomæ Hodiernis Academiarum Moribus Accommodata* (Liege, 1746; Venice, 1761; Rome, 1836; Paris, 1827, 1740, 1882). An adaptation of the great work of St. Thomas to modern times; clear, concise, and vigorous, it is one of the best expositions of Thomistic theology.

H. Kilber (†1783), T. Holtzclau (†1783), T. Neubauer (†1795). *Theologia Dogmatica, Polemica Scholastica et Moralis, seu Theologia Wirceburgensis* (Würtzburg, 1766; Paris, 1852, 3d ed. 1880, vol. 10.) These three learned Jesuits did for the theology of Suarez what Billuart had done for the Summa of St. Thomas; they adapted it to modern times.

Perrone, S. J. (†1876). *Prælectiones Theologicæ* (Naples, Louvain, 1838; Paris, 1870).

Ad. Tanquerey, S. S. *Synopsis Theologiæ Dogmaticæ Specialis* (Tournai and Baltimore, 1894). Highly commended as adapted to modern and especially American circumstances.

Ginoulhiac. *Histoire du Dogme Catholique* (Paris, 1852, 1866); probably the best Catholic work on historical theology written in our century.

J. B. Franzelin, S. J. (†1886). *De Divina Traditione et Scriptura, de Ecclesia Xti* (opus posthumum), *de Deo Uno, de Deo Trino, de verbo Incarnato, de Sacramentis in genere, de Eucharistiæ Sacramento et Sacrificio.* (Rome, 1868 ff.) The best of them is *de Divina Traditione,* in which the value of Tradition and Scripture, and their use in theology, are ably and thoroughly discussed.

Palmieri, S. J. *De Deo Creante et Elevante* (1878), *de Gratia divina actuali* (1885), *de Pœnitentia* (1879), *de Matrimonio* (1880). This last is considered the best on the subject.

Passaglia. *De Immaculato Deiparæ semper Virginis Conceptu* (*Naples*, 1855); the most exhaustive treatment of the dogma of the Immaculate Conception.

C. Mazzella, S. J. *De Religione et Ecclesia* (Roma, 1880); *de Deo Creante et Elevante* (Woodstock, 1877); *de Gratia*, (*ibid.* 1878); *de Virtutibus Infusis* (Roma, 1879). These treatises are a fair adaptation of Suarez to our own times.

De Augustinis, S. J. *De Deo Uno* (1884), *de Re Sacramentaria* (1878). The same remarks apply to these treatises which are the complement of those of Cardinal Mazzella.

Fr. Schmid. *Quæstiones Selectæ Ex Theologia Dogmatica* (Paderborn et Roma, 1891). A keenly critical examination of several theological questions not generally discussed by the standard authors.

F. Satolli. *In Summam Theologicam D. Thomæ Aq.* (5 vols. Roma, 1886–88.) This is said to be the best commentary on St. Thomas published in the present century; strong, deep, and logical, it helps the intelligent reader to understand more fully and more deeply the real mind of the Angel of the School.

F. A. Stentrup, S. J. *Prælectiones Dogmaticæ de Deo Uno* (Oenip. 1879); *de Verbo Incarnato* (1882–89).

This last work particularly is a complete and excellent treatise on the two great mysteries of the Incarnation and of the Redemption.

H. Hurter, S. J. *Theologiæ Dogmaticæ Compendium*, (8th ed. 1893); a text-book of dogma highly esteemed, especially for the richness of its materials, and the remarkable treatment of the argument of tradition.

Corluy, S. J. *Spicilegium Dogmatico-biblicum* (1884)

seems to be the necessary complement of any manual of
dogma, for it explains, with all the helps of modern exegesis, the most important texts of Scripture quoted by
theologians to prove their theses.

Migne.   *Theologiæ Cursus Completus* (Paris, 1837–45);
a vast compilation (28 vols.) containing some of the standard treatises on the various parts of dogmatic and moral
theology, which could hardly be found nowadays in any
other collection.

Wetzer und Welte's *Kirchen-Lexicon* (1847 ff.; new
edition by Kaulen, 1882, in course of publication), a vast
encyclopædia of religious knowledge, especially remarkable for its erudition and breadth of views.   Protestants
recognize that it is authoritative, fair-minded and impar-
tial to a singular degree.*   The former edition has been
translated into French by *Goschler*, Paris, 1864–68.

M. J. Scheeben.   *Dogmatik* (Freiburg, 1873–1887).   An
excellent manual of dogmatic theology in German ; leav-
ing aside controversy, the author gives to his readers a
real insight into the mysteries of faith, their inter-relations
and their bearing on Christian life.   It has been translated into French, and the first part has been translated
and abridged for English readers by Wilhelm and Scan-
nell (London, 1890) under the title, *A Manual of Catholic
Theology*.   *The Glories of Divine Grace*, of which he is
also the author, should be consulted by all on the important but difficult subject of grace.

J. H. Newman (†1890).   Among his theological works
let us mention his *Essay on the Development of Christian Doctrine*, which opened his own eyes to the light of faith, and
made him a Catholic; a most suggestive book throwing
light on all the Catholic Dogmas; *The Doctrine of Justifi-
cation*, which is a powerful refutation of the Lutheran

* *Schaff-Herzog Encyclop.*, art. *Wetzer.*

teaching on this subject; *The Arians of the Fourth Century* and *The Annotated Translation of Athanasius*, without which a study of the dogma of the Blessed Trinity can hardly be complete.

H. E. Manning (†1892). Three works of his have a bearing on dogmatic theology: *The Glories of the Sacred Heart*, *The Internal Mission of the Holy Ghost*, and *The Temporal Mission of the Holy Ghost*.   They are a clear, solid, yet simple exposition of the Catholic doctrine on these various topics.

H. N. Oxenham.   *Catholic Doctrine of the Atonement* (1865, 1881), wherein is fully explained the history of this dogma. *Catholic Eschatology and Universalism* (1876-1878), which contains an excellent refutation of the theory of probation after death.

F. W. Faber (1863).   Among his works we shall mention as more theological : *The Creator and the Creature* (1856), a beautiful description of the love of God for us and of the love we must have for Him, with a consoling view of the great mystery of predestination; *The Blessed Sacrament* (1855); *The Foot of the Cross*, or the Sorrows of Mary (1858); *Bethlehem* (1860), a treatise on the Incarnation and the Mysteries of the Sacred Infancy.   In all these works the author combines tender piety with solid learning, in a literary style which is bright and attractive.

J. B. Dalgairns.   *The Holy Communion* (Dublin, 1861, 1894); *The Devotion to the Sacred Heart* (1853); two volumes at the same time theological, historical, and devotional.

J. De Galiffet, S. J.   *The Adorable Heart of Jesus.*   This book, written in 1726, has appeared lately in an English dress (1890); it is certainly one of the most solid books on the subject it deals with.

Petitalot. *The Virgin Mother According to Theology*— Translated from the French (London, 1887). There is a good deal of solid theology in this volume, which is not always the case with books written on the Blessed Virgin.

J. Spencer Northcote. *Mary in the Gospels* (2 eḑ. London and New York, 1885); a series of Lectures on the history of the Blessed Virgin, as recorded by the Evangelists. It is an adaptation of Nicholas' *La Vierge Marie d'après l'Evangile*, and is well suited to the wants of English-speaking people.

W. Humphrey, S. J. *The One Mediator* (1890), a solid theological exposition of the doctrine of the Church on the Seven Sacraments, written in a good, attractive style.

II. WORKS ON APOLOGETICS.

Stapleton (†1598). *Principiorum fidei doctrinalium demonstratio methodica per controversias septem.* (Paris, 1579, 1620). The main purpose of the author is to prove the existence of an infallible authority in the Church. A second edition of this work, *Principiorum fidei doctrinalium Relectio scholastica et compendiaria,* is, though abridged, more highly esteemed than the first.

Duperron (†1618). *Traité du Sacrement de l'Eucharistie ; Réplique au Roi de la Grande Bretagne, etc.* (Paris, 1620, 1622). The former is a solid refutation of the objections against the Blessed Eucharist; the latter, a powerful demonstration of the duty incumbent on all Christians of joining the visible society which alone deserves the name of Catholic Church.

Roberti Bellarmini, S. J. (†1621). *Disputationes de Controversiis Fidei.* (*Ingolstadt,* 1586; Venice, 1596; Paris 1618; Cologne, 1619; Prague, 1721, with the additions of Ebermann; Paris, 1870–74). Probably the most exhaustive work of controversy ever published.   ,

St. Francis of Sales (†1622). *Controversies*, translated into English by H. B. Mackey, O. S. B. (Vol. 3 of the English edition of his complete works). Clear, solid and gently persuasive.

Pascal (†1662). *Pensées.* (Best French edition, Tours, 1873, a part of the collection: *Les Apologistes du Christianisme au XVII. siècle ;* English translat. by Wight, New York, a new one by C. Kegan Paul, London). An unfinished work, but very suggestive, the purpose of which is to demonstrate the insufficiency of reason in religious matters, and the necessity of revelation.

Bossuet (†1704). *Discours sur l'Histoire Universelle,* an historical demonstration of the divinity of Christianity. *Histoire des Variationes des Eglises Protestantes,* wherein the falsity of Protestantism is proved from its manifold doctrinal changes. *Exposition de la doctrine de l'Eglise Catholique sur les matières de controverse ;* a clear, concise *exposé* of the Catholic doctrine on matters of controversy, which may greatly help toward removing prejudice—translated into English, New York.

Fénelon (†1715). *Lettres sur la Réligion ;* a brief but excellent demonstration of the divinity of religion. *De Summi Pontificis Auctoritate ;* a clear demonstration of the infallibility of the S. Pontiff.

Guénée (†1803). *Lettres de quelques Juifs* . . . (Paris, 1769, 1857, etc.; translated into English by *Lefaun,* Dublin, 1877). This is the wittiest and strongest reply to Voltaire's attacks on the Old Testament; may be still used against the unbelievers who, like Paine and Ingersoll, repeat the same objections.

P. Ballerini (†1769). *De Vi ac Ratione Primatus Rom. Pontificum* (Verona, 1768, Torino, 1822; also in *Migne's* Theol. Curs. t. 3). The author explains, with great erudition, the nature and extent of Papal supremacy, against

Febronius, and proves conclusively the infallibility of the Roman Pontiff in definitions of faith.

Hooke (†1796). *Religionis Naturalis Revelatæ Principia* (Paris, 1752; Venice, 1763; partly inserted in *Migne's* Theol. Curs. vol. 2.) A classical work, solidly proving the existence of God, the necessity of a religion, the divinity of Christianity and of the Catholic Church.

Joseph de Maistre (†1821). *Du Pape* (1819); *Soirées de St. Petersbourg* (1821); a lucid and eloquent, though at times declamatory, demonstration of the practical utility of the Papal power.

J. Milner (†1826). *The End of Religious Controversy ;* a popular book written in the shape of letters to vindicate the Catholic rule of faith, to prove that the Roman Catholic Church is the only true Church, and to meet the objections of her opponents.

Chateaubriand (1848). *Génie du Christianisme* (1802, translated into English by *C. White*, Baltimore, 1856); a masterpiece of literary art, more famous for its poetical description of the beauties of Christianity than for its erudition.

D. Rock. *Hierurgia, or the Holy Sacrifice of the Mass* (London, 1833, 1893); containing, besides an explanation of the ceremonies of the Liturgy, learned dissertations on the doctrine of the Eucharist, as a sacrifice and a sacrament; on the invocation of saints, on Purgatory, etc.

J. Balmès (1848). *El Protestantismo comparado con el Catolicismo.* (Barcelona, 1841; English translation, Baltimore, 1851, *Protestantism and Catholicity Compared in their Effects on the Civilization of Europe.*) A book mostly historical, showing, by a review of modern civilization, that the influence of Catholicity has been far superior to that of Protestantism. *Letters to a Sceptic on Religious Matters ;* an application of the rules of logic to religious questions, extremely valuable to refute the fallacies of modern unbelievers.

F. Martin, *De l'avenir du Protestantisme et du Catholicisme* (Paris, 1869); a book which is the complement of that of Balmès, inasmuch as it explains, among other things, why Protestant nations seem to be more prosperous than Catholic countries.

Moehler (1838). *Symbolik* (Mayence, 1832; seventh edition, 1884; translated into English by *J. R. Robertson :* "Symbolism, or the Doctrinal Differences Between Catholics and Protestants"; London, 1843; New York, 1844, 1894).

F. P. Kenrick (†1863). *The Primacy of the Holy See* (1837; third edition, New York, 1848). One of the best works on the Primacy.

H. D. Lacordaire, O. P. (†1861). *Conférences de N. D. de Paris et de Toulouse* (Paris, 1835–54; most of them have been translated into English by H. Langdon, London, New York, 1870–75). One of the most eloquent apologies of Christianity, well adapted to our own times, insisting especially on the moral effects produced by the Catholic teaching on society and the individual.

F. M. J. Moigno, *Les Splendeurs de la Foi.* (Paris, 1879–1885, 5 vols.) An exhaustive treatise to show the perfect accord of revelation with science, of faith with reason. The first and last volumes will be found particularly valuable.

J. B. Malou (†1864). *La Lecture de la S. Bible en langue vulgaire ;* a work of great erudition, refuting the principles advanced by the Bible Societies with regard to the reading of Holy Scripture; *L'Immaculée Conception de la B. Vierge Marie* (Brussels, 1857); an able and vigorous defence of the dogma of the Immaculate Conception.

N. Wiseman (1865). *Lectures on the Connection Between*

Science and Revealed Religion (London, 1836, 1853; New York, Baltimore, 1852); a masterly work, still valuable in its leading principles, though some of its applications have lost their original force on account of the advance of scientific research. *Lectures on the Principal Doctrines and Practices of the Church* (London, 1836; Baltimore, 1862, etc.); particularly deep and strong are the lectures on the rule of Faith and Transubstantiation. *Lectures on the Real Presence* (London, 1836; Baltimore, 1871, etc.); a masterpiece of exegesis; one of the strongest biblical arguments written in behalf of the Catholic dogma of the Real Presence.

J. H. Newman (†1890). *Apologia pro Vita Sua* (1864); *Loss and Gain* (1848); *Difficulties of Anglicans* (1850); *Lectures on the Present Position of Catholics in England* (1851). For depth of thought, vigor of logic and purity of style they are unrivalled. The second volume of *Difficulties of Anglicanism* contains the author's *Letter to Pusey*, which is one of the best works we have in English on the Blessed Virgin

H. E. Manning (†1892). *Petri Privilegium*. (London, 1871); an historical demonstration of the infallibility of the Roman Pontiff, and a lucid explanation of the same doctrine as defined by the Council of the Vatican. The author's *Religio Viatoris* is a succinct, but extremely logical book, pointing out the way to Catholicism.

Bishop Ullathorne. *The Endowments of Man* (London, 1888); a course of lectures on the nature, origin, fall, restoration and end of man.

O. Brownson's (†1876) *Complete Works* (Detroit, 1882–87).

W. G. Ward (†1882). *The Philosophy of Theism* (London, 1884); a series of essays against the various forms of contemporary atheism or agnosticism, wherein the difficulties raised by Mill and Huxley are frankly met, and vigorously refuted.   .

P. Murray, *De Ecclesia Christi* (Dublin, 1860-66); a very complete treatise on the Church, remarkable for its solid refutation of the many objections raised by Protestants, and the developments given to the traditional argument.

Wallon, *De la Croyance due à l'Evangile* (Paris, 1858, 1866); a book full of erudition, critical and well written, probably the strongest refutation among Catholics, of the modern attacks against the historical value of the Gospel.

Nicholas (†1888). *Etudes Philosophiques sur le Christianisme* (Paris, 1844); a philosophical and historical demonstration of the divinity of Christianity. *La Nativité de N. S. Jésus Christ* (transl. into English, London, 1865); a new demonstration of the divinity of our Lord, and especially a reply to Rénan.

Ch. E. Freppel (†1891). *Les Apologistes Chrétiens au Deuxième Siècle* (Paris, 1860, 3d ed. 1866); an attractive study of the Christian Apologists of the second century, with the purpose of refuting modern infidelity with the weapons of the Fathers;—*Examen critique de la Vie de M. Rénan* (Paris, 1863); *Confrences sur la divinité de J. C.* (Paris, 1863; Engl. transl., London and New York); refutations of Rénan's life of Jesus and an historical demonstration of the divinity of our Lord.

F. Hettinger. *Lehrbuch der Fundamentaltheologie oder Apologetik* (Freiburg, 1879, 1888); *Apologie des Christenthum's* (Freiburg, 1862-67, 6th ed. 1885). The purpose of the writer is to show the agreement of Christian faith with all that is true in the domain of reason, to correct erroneous theories, and heal the wounds which error causes in souls; which is done with a great deal of erudition and eloquence. The *Apology of Christianity* has been translated into French (Paris, 1869), and a part of it, *Natural Re-*

ligion, has been adapted for English readers by H. S. Bowden. (London and New York, 1890).

P. Schanz. *Apologie des Christenthum's* (Freiburg, 1887–89; transl. into English by *M. F. Glancey* and *V. J. Schobel*, 1890–92); a complete course of apologetics, full of erudition up to date, truly scientific, but somewhat didactic.

P. Weiss, O. P. *Apologie des Christenthum's vom Standpunkt der Sitte und Kultur* (Freiburg, 1889). This is a truly new and original work, showing from historical facts the influence of revelation on morals and civilization.

Félix, S. J. (†1892). *Le Progrès par le Christianisme;* a series of Conferences preached in the pulpit of N. Dame (Paris, 1856–1864), to prove that Christianity is the best means of intellectual, moral, and social progress. One volume (1864) is devoted to proving the divinity of Jesus Christ against Rénan.

Monsabré, O. P. *Introduction au Dogme Catholique* (1865); *Exposition au Dogme Catholique* (Paris, 1873–90). The former series is a substantial and eloquent demonstration of the Christian revelation against the rationalists of our own time. The latter is an exposition of the Catholic dogmas, in which the author follows St. Thomas step by step.

Mgr. Bougaud (†1888). *Le Christianisme et les temps Présents* (Paris, 1871–85); a work beautifully written, making Christianity attractive by adapting it to the needs of our generation. His demonstration of the divinity of Jesus Christ is a masterpiece.

Dechamps (1883). *Entretiens sur la Demonstration Catholique de la Revelation ; La Question Religieuse resolue par les Faits.* Two works very suggestive, wherein, from a deep analysis of the human mind, the author proves how perfectly the Catholic Church harmonizes with our intellectual needs.

Brugère, S. S. (†1888). *De Vera Religione, de Ecclesia Xti* (Paris, 1878); a truly original work, full of erudition, rich in quotation and reference.

Gondal, S. S. *La Religion* (1893), *Le Surnaturel* (1894); the beginning of a series of volumes destined to bring up to date the Christian demonstration, and refute the latest attacks of modern unbelief.

Palmieri, S. J. *De Romano Pontifice* (1891); one of the best treatises on the subject.

De Groat, O. P. *Summa apologetica de Ecclesia catholica ad mentem S. Thomæ* (Ratisbonne, 1890); a very good treatment of this important subject, up to date, and extremely logical.

L' Abbé de Broglie. *Problèmes et conclusions de l'Histoire des religions* (2d ed. 1886); a comparative study of the main religions still existing in the world.

T. W. Allies. *The Formation of Christendom*, consisting of a series of seven volumes, which together with *A Life's Decision*, make up a strong historical demonstration of the Primacy of the Holy See.

T. Livius, C. SS. R. *S. Peter, Bishop of Rome* (London and New York, 1888); a luminous and fairly exhaustive treatment of the question of S. Peter's Roman Episcopate. *The B. Virgin in the Fathers of the first Six Centuries*, a work of great erudition, in which we hear the combined voices of the Fathers united in speaking the praise of Mary.

Luke Rivington. *Authority* (London, 1888); *Dependence* (London, 1889); *The Primitive Church and the See of S. Peter* (London, 1894); demonstrating that the Primacy of the H. See was accepted from the early times.

Jaugey (†1894). *Dictionnaire apologétique de la Foi Catholique* (1889); a good summary of the latest results of Catholic Apologetics.

I. T. Hecker, C. S. P. (†1888). *Questions of the Soul* (New York, 1855); *The Aspirations of the Soul* (1857); *The Church and the Age ;* written by one who knew well the American mind, proving that the Catholic Church alone satisfactorily answers the demands of the human soul with regard to its destiny and the means to attain it.

A. F. Hewitt, C. S. P. *The Problems of the Age* (1868) ; attempt to show that the leading problems of the age find a happy solution in the Catholic Church.

J. Gibbons, Cardinal. *Our Christian Heritage* (1889) ; *The Faith of Our Fathers* (1876).

James Kent Stone, now Father Fidelis. *The Invitation Heeded* (1870); the solid reasons why, in answer to Pope Pius IX's. appeal, he joined the Catholic Church.

J. Thein, *Christian Anthropology* (New York, 1892) ; a fair treatment of all the questions which pertain to the origin, nature, antiquity and destiny of man.

J. A. Zahm, C. S. C., *Bible, Science and Faith* (Baltimore 1894) ; a series of essays reprinted from the *American Eccles. Review* and the *Amer. Cath. Quart. Review*, in which the author, who is well versed in the sciences, shows how the Mosaic Hexaëmeron, the Noachian Deluge and the biblical chronology may be reconciled with the latest data of science. *Evolution and Dogma* (Chicago, 1896) is a continuation of above.

Didon, O. P. *Belief in the Divinity of Jesus Christ* ₍London and New York, 1894) ; contrasting the futility of the reasons for which unbelievers deny the divinity of Our Lord with the solid grounds on which our faith rests ; a lucid and eloquent discussion.

Lambert. *Notes on Ingersoll ; Tactics of Infidels ;* witty, trenchant and popular refutations of the fallacies of R. Ingersoll.

DEPARTMENT OF LITURGY.

I.—INDISPENSABLE BOOKS.

First, The *Missale Romanum.* The *Missal for the Laity*, Burns and Oates, London, is an English translation of the Roman Missal. Contains the Masses of the principal feasts.

Second, The *Breviarium Romanum.* A superb English version, in 2 vols., has been published by the Marquis of Bute.

Third, The *Rituale Romanum. Notes on the Rubrics,* by O'Kane, is a valuable explanation and commentary for English readers.

A *Calendarium* or *Ordo divini officii,* which indicates day by day what Mass is to be celebrated and what Office to be recited.

II.—BOOKS VERY USEFUL.

The principal and more useful extracts are the *Officium Defunctorum,* with musical notes to serve at Masses and Offices for the dead ; the *Graduale* and the *Vesperale* likewise with plain chant notes.

The *Pontificale Romanum* will be found handy for episcopal visits and functions. The *Martyrologium Romanum* is the official list of saints.

Ceremonial of the Church in the United States. The work was first published as an official handbook of liturgy by order of the First Plenary Council of Baltimore.

As a text-book on liturgy, the best undoubtedly and the most complete for its size is the *Sacræ Liturgiæ Praxis* of De Herdt, a work universally known and esteemed. Wapelhorst's *Compendium Liturgiæ Sacræ* is shorter.

A thorough commentary on the Ritual is Baruffaldi, *Ad Rituale Romanum Commentaria,* but a more accessible one is the well-known *Notes* of O'Kane *on the Rubrics of the Roman Ritual.* For lay people, *Order and Ceremonial of the Mass*, Oakeley ; *Hierurgia*, Rock ; *La Messe* and *Les Saints de la Messe*, Rohault de Fleury ; *Liturgy for the Laity*, O'Donnell ; *Catholic Worship*, Gisler.

<h3 style="text-align:center">III.—OTHER HELPS IN LITURGY.</h3>

The *Ceremoniale Episcoporum*, with its commentary, the *Praxis Pontificalis* of De Herdt, or the shorter *Commentaria* on the *Pontifical* and the *Ceremonial* by Proto, and also the *Rites of Sacerdotal Ordination*, translated by Dr. Lynch, and of *Episcopal Consecration*, translated by Rev. J. H. McMahon. The *Manuale Sacrarum Ceremoniarum* of Martinucci, the fullest and most accurate delineator of sacred ceremonies. The *Decreta authentica S. Congregationis Rituum*, as edited either by Gardellini or his alphabetical imitator, W. Muhlbauer.   In the same connection occurs Falise's *Liturgiæ Practicæ Compendium* and his *S. Congregationis Decreta authentica.*   A very convenient book for reference on the same decrees is Adone's *Synopsis Canonica Liturgica*, while for rubrics in general the *Bibliotheca Canonica*, etc., of Ferraris, is full of information.   Such, too, on the Mass is the exhaustive work of Benedict XIV., *de Sacrificio Missæ.*

The *Praxis Synodalis* of Bishop Messmer for the proper celebrations of councils and synods.

The *Liturgical Year* of Dom Gueranger, the great restorer of liturgical unity in France, who expounds with so much love the literal and spiritual sense of the sacred ceremonies, together with their history and variations.   The *History of the Mass*, by O'Brien.

<h2 style="text-align:center">DEPARTMENT OF CHURCH HISTORY.</h2>

De Smedt, S. J. *Introductio Generalis ad Historiam Ec-*

clesiasticam, 1 vol., 1876. The classical Catholic work on the subject by the great Bollandist—a work, however, more for the student than the general reader of Church history.

De Smedt, S. J. *Principes de la Critique Historique.* 1 vol., 1883. A most suggestive book for the worker in Church history, and a book, too, of very general interest.

Feller. *Biographie Universelle.* Many different editions. Not a critical work, but very useful for its short biographies of men not usually noticed in English or American publications of this kind.

Werner, S. J. *Orbis Terrarum Catholicus.* 1 vol., 1890. —*Atlas Missionum.* 1 vol. An ecclesiastical atlas.

Wetzer & Welte. *Kirchen Lexicon.* (2d edition, 1879.) The new edition of this great work in German was begun by Card. Hergenrœther, and is being continued by Prof. Kaulen. It is being translated also into French.

MANUALS OF CHURCH HISTORY.

Alzog. 3 vols. The best in English.

Darras. 4 vols. Readable, but unreliable.

Hergenrœther. 3 vols. As yet only in German and French. Notable for bibliographies.

Gilmartin. 2 vols. Down to the Reformation.

Berti. *Eccles. Historiae Breviarium.* 2 vols. Continued by Lopez down to 1879.

LARGER HISTORIES OF THE CHURCH.

Rohrbacher. Several editions. In French and German. 14 vols. with an index, and 2 vols. suppl. annals.

Darras. 44 vols. In French.

Jungmann. *Dissertationes Selectæ.* 7 vols. 1880–87. This is not a complete history of the Church, but it covers most of the questions of Church history.

Hefelè. *History of the Councils.* 10 (12) vols. Several editions. Original in German. Translated into French. The 1st vol. in English in Clark's Theological Library, (4 vols.) Invaluable as a reference work.

Martigny. *Dictionnaire d'antiquités chrétiennes.* 1 vol. Edition of 1877.

WORKS ON SPECIAL PERIODS.

Eusebius, Socrates, Sozomen, Theodoret,—each forms a volume in the *Bohn Library* series of *English translations.*

Acta Martyrum. Edited by Dom Ruinart. Last edition Ratisbonne, 1859.

Allies. *The Formation of Christendom.* 2 vols. A popular edition in 1 vol. has been published. The series forms a valuable contribution to Church history : *Holy See and the Wandering of the Nations ; Peter's Rock in Mohammed's Flood ; The Monastic Life.*

Palma. *Prælectiones Historicæ.* Contains arguments on the chief topics of Church history down to the sixteenth century.

Allard. *Histoire des Persécutions.* 5 vols. The classical modern book on the Persecutions.

Northcote & Brownlow's *Roma Sotteranea.* 3 vols.

De Smedt, S. J. *Dissertationes Selectæ in I^{am.} Ætatem Hist. Eccles.* 1 vol. 1876.

Lilly. *Chapters of European History.* 2 vols.

Fouard. *The Lives of St. Peter and St. Paul.*

De Broglie. *L'Eglise et l'Empire Romain au IV. Siècle.* 6 vols.

S. Liguori. *History of Heresies.* 2 vols.

Mrs. Hope's *The Conversion of the Teutonic Races.* 2 vols.

The works of *Ozanam* (on the Franks and Germans and

Middle Ages generally), of *Lingard* (on the Anglo-Saxons), of *Montalembert* (the Monks of the West).

Lives of S. Augustine (by a Priest of the Mission), *S. Patrick* (by F. Morris), *S. Gregory Great* (by Abbot Snow), *S. Boniface* (by Mrs. Hope).

Parsons' *Studies in Church History.* 2 vols. Takes up disputed questions.

ON THE MIDDLE AGES.

Digby. *Mores Catholici.* 4 vols. in last edition.   Of this work Adams in his Manual of Historical Literature says: " A work of remarkable erudition in sharp contrast with the hasty generalizations of Lecky."

Drane. *Christian Schools and Scholars.* 1 vol.

Christophe. *Histoire de la Papauté pendant le XIV. Siècle.* 3 vols.

Pastor. *History of the Popes* (from the end of the Middle Ages). Three vols. in German. First two volumes of the German have been thus far translated into English by Fr. Autrobus, in four volumes, bringing the work up to 1484.

Hergenrœther. *The Church and State.* 2 vols. in English translation.   The ablest apology for the secular history of the Papacy.

BIOGRAPHIES.

St. Gregory VII.   Voigt.

St. Bernard, by Ratisbonne (Cath.).   Latest, 2 vols. Abbé Vacandard.

St. Anselm.   Rule.

St. Edmund.   Wallace.

St. Thomas Becket, by Morris.

Innocent III., by Hurter in German and French.

St. Dominic, by Drane.

St. Francis, L'Abbé Monnier.

St. Thomas of Aquin.   2 vols. by Vaughan, notable
for its account of early Scholasticism.   More recently by
Kavanagh, O.P.

Albert the Great, Sighart.

St. Catherine of Siena.   2 vols.   Drane.

THE PERIOD OF THE REFORMATION.

Janssens.   *The History of the German People from the
Close of the Middle Ages.*   8 vols.   This great classic, one
of the best works of the century, has been translated
from the German into French.   An English translation
is now announced.

Spalding.   History of the Reformation.   2 vols.   Answer to D'Aubigné.

Balmes.   *Protestantism and Catholicity Compared.*   1 vol.

Pallavicini, S.J.   *The Council of Trent.*   In Latin, Ital-
ian, and French.

Gasquet, O.S.B.   *Henry VIII. and the English Monas-
teries.*   2 vols.

Parsons.   *Some Lies and Errors of History.*   1 vol.   A
popular refutation.

Bridgett.   *Blunders and Forgeries.*   Referring to English History only.

BIOGRAPHIES.

Life of Card. Ximenes.   Hefelè, translated into English.

Life of Savonarola.   2 vols.   Villari in English translation.   To be read with caution.

Life of Luther.   Audin ("full of errors."—Alzog).

Life of St. Charles Borromeo.

Life of Bl. Thomas More.   F. Bridgett.

Life of Bl. John Fisher.   F. Bridgett.

Life of F. Gerard (the Gunpowder Plot). Brother Foley.

Life of M. Olier. Edw. Healey Thompson.

Life of St. Francis de Sales.

Life of Sixtus V. Hubner (in French).

Life of St. Ignatius.

Life of St. Francis Xavier.

Marshall. *Christian Missions.* 2 vols. Has been charged with exaggeration, which does not, however, deprive the work of its value as a comparative index of Catholic and Protestant methods.

J. G. Shea. *History of the Catholic Church in the United States.* 4 vols.

Manning. *England and Christendom.*

Newman. *Historical Sketches, etc.*

REVIEWS.

Dublin Review.

Revue des Questions Historiques.

DEPARTMENT OF CANON LAW.

Corpus Juris Canonici. This is the fundamental source, and a requisite of every canon law library. There are many critical editions made after the Roman of 1582 (5 vol.), any of which will serve the purpose of reference. As one of the best, we would recommend the *Edit. Lipsiens. secund. post Æmil. Lud. Richteri curas instruxit Æmilius Friedberg. II. part* (*Leipsic, 1879–1881*). If it is possible to procure an old edition with glosses, the opportunity should not be neglected.

Concilium Tridentinum.—Pallottini. Collectio Omnium Conclusionum S. Concil. Trid., 1564 ad 1860. (Romæ typ. S. C. de Prop. Fide).

Collectanea S. Congregationis de Propag. Fide. This contains Decrees, Instructions and Rescripts, for missionary countries. The best edition is that of 1893.

Acta Sanctæ Sedis. A periodical publication, which gives the new decrees of the S. Congregations. It is well to procure the volumes of the last few years, for reference to recent decisions.

Laurin, Fr. *Introductio in Corpus Juris Canon.* cum brevi Introduct. in Corpus Juris Civil. (Freiburg, 1889). One of the best among numerous manuals, as an aid to a just estimate and right interpretation of the foregoing sources.

Decreta I., II., III., Conciliorum Balt. The Decrees of the three plenary Councils held at Baltimore, which form the special Canon Law of the Roman Catholic Church in the United States. To these should be added the Decrees of various Provincial and Diocesan Synods held throughout the country at various times.

Reiffenstuel, Anal. *Jus Can. Univers.* juxta titulos libr. V. decretal. 3 vol. (Monach. 1702.—Rom. 1829 et iter.—7 vol. 4to., Paris, 1870.)

Schmalzgrueber. *Jus Eccl. Univers.* 5 vol. (Ingolst. 1726.—Romæ, 1843–1845).

Angelis, Phil. de. *Prælectiones Juris Can.* 3 vol. not complete. Romæ, 1877–1880. Edit. nov. 4 vol. 1888–1891).

Santi, Fr. *Prælectiones Juris Canon.* juxta ordinem Decret. Greg. IX., libri. V., (Ratisbonæ 1886).

On special topics of Canon Law it is well to consult the following partial commentaries :

Ferraris, L. *Prompta Bibliotheca Canonica.* 8 vol. (Migne. Paris, 1852–1858). There are numerous other editions of seven or eight volumes.

Benedictus XIV. *De Synodo Diœcesana.* A work almost constantly referred to in matters of ecclesiastical discipline. Numerous editions. Among the complete works of the Pontiff. (Prati, 1844).

Bouix, S. *Institutiones Juris Canonici.* There are nine tracts in 12 vol. (Paris 1852-1870.)

Smith, S. B. *Elements of Ecclesiastical Law.* This work is of special use to American students, inasmuch as it has been written with reference to the existing discipline of the Church in the United States. It embraces Vol. I., *Ecclesiastical Persons;* Vol. II., *Ecclesiastical Trials;* Vol. III., *Ecclesiastical Punishments.* Nine editions. (New York, 1878-1893.)

Vering, F. *Kirchenrecht* (Freiburg, Br., 1893).

Smith, S. B. *The Marriage Process in the United States,* (New York, 1893).—*New Procedure in Criminal and Disciplinary Causes;* an explanation of the Instr. S. C. "Cum Magnopere" (New York).

Messmer, S. G., present Bishop of Green Bay, who edited *Fr. Droste's* work on *Canonical Procedure* in Disciplinary and Criminal Cases of Clerics. Likewise an excellent commentary on the instruction "Cum Magnopere" (New York).

Konings, A. *Commentarium in Facultates Apostolicas* quæ Episcopis et Vicar. Apost. concedi solent. The third edition by Rev. Jos. Putzer, C.SS.R., entirely remodels the work and brings it up to date (Ilchester, 1894).

Péries, G. *Code de Procédure Canonique dans les Causes Matrimoniales* (Paris, 1894).

It is needless to mention that the *Acta et Decreta* of the Second and Third Plenary Councils of Baltimore are essential books.

Nilles, Nicolai, S.J. *Commentaria in Concilium Pl. Baltim. III.,* ex Prælectionibus Academicis excerpta. (Œniponte, 1888.)

DEPARTMENT OF PHILOSOPHY.

Tongiorgi. *Institutiones Philosophicæ*, 3 vols. without Ethics.

Zigliara (Card.). *Summa Philosophica*, 3 vols. with Ethics.

San Severino. *Philosophia Christiana*, 7 vols.

Urraburu. *Logica, Ontologia, Cosmologia*, 3 large vols. 8vo.

Cathrein. *Philosophia Moralis*, 1 vol.; *Moral Philosophie*, 2 vols. (German); *Socialism*, 1 vol. (an English translation of a portion of the preceding work).

Pesch. *Institutiones Philosophicæ*.

Ming. *Data of Modern Ethics*, 1 vol.

Catholic Philosophy. Stonyhurst Series, 7 vols., *viz :—*
Logic. Clarke.

First Principles of Knowledge. Rickaby, John.

General Metaphysics. Rickaby, John.

Psychology. Maher.

Natural Theology. Bœdder.

Moral Philosophy. Rickaby, Joseph.

Political Economy. Devas.

Harper. *The Metaphysics of the School*, 3 vols.

Balmes. *Fundamental Philosophy*, 2 vols.

Reeb. *Thesaurus Philosophorum*, 1 vol., (a small pocket dictionary of philosophical distinctions and axioms).

Mivart. *Philosophical Catechism*, 47 small pages.

Zigliara is deep, incisive—a true metaphysician, whom Leo XIII. recognized and appointed Præfectus Studiorum of the Catholic Universities.

San Severino, working in line with Liberatore, gives an extended and lucid exposition of the philosophy of St. Thomas, and a complete refutation of the philosophical errors of ancient and modern times.

LaHousse and Van der Aa touch all the questions of

the day. LaHousse is valuable as presenting in full the scholastic method of disputation. Van der Aa is compact and constructive, building securely upon well-laid foundations.

Harper's " Metaphysics of the School " is held by some to be the most important work on pure metaphysics written during this century.

In the " Cosmologia " of Urraburu we have an exhaustive treatment of the metaphysics of matter, and of all the subjects that are usually brought under Cosmology.

The " Stonyhurst Series," the only complete course of philosophy in the English language, is new, fresh, and " up to date." Though it contains no separate treatise on Cosmology, nearly all the questions of Cosmology are touched upon in the Psychology and Natural Theology.

HISTORY OF PHILOSOPHY.

One volume only, of the valuable work of Stœckl has been translated into English. It is thoroughly reliable.

SACRED SCRIPTURE.

INTRODUCTION.—Introduction to the Sacred Scriptures in a series of dissertations, critical, heremeneutical and historical, by the Rev. Joseph Dixon, D. D., Professor of Sacred Scripture and Hebrew in the Royal College of St. Patrick, Maynooth.

Introd. hist. et critica, A. Cornely. 4 vol. " Historica et critica Introductio in U. T. Libros Sacros," by R. Cornely, S. J. (Parisiis, 1885–1886), at present the most complete and satisfactory work on the subject.

Manuel Biblique—F. Vigouroux and L. Bacuez, 4 vol. edit. VIII., 1891–92 (Paris, 1891–1892).

Introduction to the Sacred Scriptures by the Rev. John MacDevitt, D. D., Professor of the Introduction to Script-

ure, in All-Hallows Foreign Missionary College, Dublin
(Dublin & New York, 1889).

Chapters in Bible Study, by the Rev. H. J. Heuser,
Prof. of Exegesis, St. Charles' Seminary, Overbrook, Pa.
(N. Y., 1895).

Institutio de Interpretatione Bibliorum, F. X. Patrizi
(Romæ, 1862).

The Four Gospels Examined and Vindicated on Catholic
Principles, by M. Heiss (Milwaukee, 1863).

Tatian's Diatessaron, by M. Maher, S. J.

La Bible et les Decouvertes Modernes, by F. Vigouroux
(Paris, 1884 ff).

Biblical Antiquities, Jahn (Oxford, 1836).

A Day in the Temple, Maas.

The Gentile and the Jew in the Courts of the Temple of
Christ, Doellinger (London, 1862).

First Age of the Church, Doellinger (London, 1867).

Saint Peter and the First Years of Christianity, Griffith's
translation of Fouard (New York, 1892).

St. Paul and his Missions (New York, 1894).

Life of Jesus Christ, Coleridge, Fouard, Didon, Maas,
and by the Protestant writers Edersheim, Keim, Geikie,
Weiss, and others.

Description géographique, historique et archéologique
de la Palestine, Guérin.

Judée (3 vols).   (Paris, 1860–1869);

Samarie, 2 vols.   (Paris, 1874–1875);

Galilée, 2 vols.   (Paris, 1880).

La Terre Sainte, by De Hamme (Jerusalem and Paris,
1887).

Lexicon Biblicum in quo explicantur Vulgatæ vocabula
et phrases (Augustæ Taurinorum, 1866).

Calmet's Bible Dictionary, trans. by Horstman.

Dictionnaire de la Bible—F. Vigouroux (Dictionnaire de la Bible, Paris). Nine parts have been issued thus far.

Concordantiarum Manuale (smaller).

Thesaurus Biblicus, or Hand-book of Scripture References, Lambert (Waterloo, N. Y., 1880).

The Divine Armory of Holy Scripture, by Vaughan (Catholic Book Exchange, 1894).

Commentaries: Good commentaries upon the Old and New Testaments have been written by Hugo a S. Caro, Nicolaus of Lyra, Cornelius a Lapide, Emanuel Sa, Menochius, Tirinus, Mariana, Calmet, Allioli, Loch and Reischle. The *Dublin Review*, in announcing Mossman's English Translation of part of a Lapide's Commentary (SS. Matthew and Mark's Gospels in 3 vols.; St. John's Gospel and three Epistles in 2 vols.; St. Luke's Gospel in 1 vol.), said: " It is the most erudite, the richest, and altogether the completest commentary on the Holy Scriptures that has ever been written."

Cursus S. Scripturæ, issued by the German Jesuit Fathers, and the French series of Commentaries, now complete, which numbers 29 volumes, and counts among its authors Trochon, Crelier, Lesetre, Fillion, Drach, and other writers of great merit. The Latin series by the German Jesuits is not yet finished ; but Cornely has thus far contributed four vols. of an Introduction, and Commentaries on the Epistle of the Corinthians I. and II., and on the Epistle to the Galatians ; Hummelauer has furnished Commentaries on the Books of Judges and Ruth, and also on Kings I. and II.; Gietmann has written on Ecclesiastes and the Canticle of Canticles; Knabenbauer has explained the Gospels of Matthew, Mark, and Luke, the Book of Job, the Prophecies of Isaias, Jeremias, Baruch, Daniel, Ezechiel, and the Minor Prophets. These two Catholic Bible series compare very favorably with either the Speaker's Commentary or the Cambridge Bible. In fact, this last series appears very elementary alongside the above Catholic Commentaries. The English Jesuits have in hand a commentary in English which is announced for immediate publication.

Christ in type and Prophecy, Maas. 2 vols. (New York, 1892–1895).

Le Livre de Job, Le Hir (Paris, 1873).

Les Psaumes tráduits de l'Hebreu en Latin, LeHir (Paris, 1876).

Commentary on the Holy Gospels, by Maldonatus, trans. into English by Davie (Dublin, 1876).

Exposition of the Gospels, McEvilly's (Dublin, 1876).

The Life of Jesus Christ According to the Gospel History (St. Louis, 1892).

Gospel of St. Matthew, McCarthy (Dublin, 1877).

Commen. in Joannem, Corluy (Gandavi, 1882).

Commen. in Acta, Beelen (Lovanii, 1850).

St. Paul's and Catholic Epistles and the Acts, McEvilly (Lugduni, 1612).

Epist. ad Romanos, Beelen.

Epist. ad Galatas, Palmieri.

Familiar Introduction to the Study of the Sacred Scriptures, Formby.

The Written Word, Humphrey. The second edition bears the title, The Sacred Scriptures.

Errata in the Protestant Bible, Ward.

Epistles and Gospels throughout the Year, McCarthy.

THE END.

INDEX

INDEX.

www.ingramcontent.com/pod-product-compliance
Lightning Source LLC
Chambersburg PA
CBHW031443280326
41927CB00038B/1576